Get the Happiness Habit

Get the Happiness Habit

How You Can Choose Your
Steps to a Happy Life

Christine Webber

Hodder & Stoughton
LONDON SYDNEY AUCKLAND

First published in Great Britain in 2000

The right of Christine Webber to be identified as
the Author of the Work has been asserted by her in accordance
with the Copyright, Designs and Patents Act 1988.

10 9 8 7 6 5 4 3 2 1

British Library Cataloguing in Publication Data
A record for this book is available from the British Library

ISBN 0 340 74593 2

Typeset in Caslon by Avon DataSet Ltd,
Bidford-on-Avon, Warwickshire

Printed and bound in Great Britain by
Bookmarque Ltd, Croydon, Surrey

The paper and board used in this paperback are natural recyclable products
made from wood grown in sustainable forests. The manufacturing processes
conform to the environmental regulations of the country of origin.

Hodder & Stoughton Ltd
A Division of Hodder Headline
338 Euston Road
London NW1 3BH
www.madaboutbooks.com

To my lovely husband, David Delvin,
who is not responsible for my happiness,
but who contributes to it more than I can say.

Contents

Acknowledgments

Warmest thanks go to two fabulous women in my life: Judith Longman at Hodder, who asked me to write this book, and my agent, Ali Gunn, who encouraged me throughout.

I'd also like to thank my tutors, Maggie Rogers and Sylvia Wright, for broadening my mind and experience; and my friend, Jasmit Sodhi, for reading my manuscript, and saying all the right things!

In addition I wish to thank my clients past and present, for everything they've taught me.

1

Introduction to Happiness: What Happiness Is – and What It Isn't

Suppose, for a moment, that you suddenly heard you were going to die today. It's hard to imagine what conflicting emotions would race round your brain at this dreadful and unexpected news, but I expect that panic, anger, disbelief and distress would all be in there somewhere. You'd probably also feel deeply anxious about putting your affairs in order, and you'd almost certainly want to see, or telephone, as many friends and family members as possible.

But after the initial shock, I feel sure that your predominant feeling would be one of sadness – sadness that you had wasted so much of your life in being miserable, when you might have been happy instead.

And why am I so sure about that? Because during my years as

an advice-columnist I've had countless letters from people going through major crises. And almost all of my correspondents have expressed huge regret at failing to live life to the full before tragedy overtook them.

Take Diane, for example. She wrote to say that her husband, Jim, had had a stroke. His progress back to fitness was painfully slow, and Diane was grief-stricken at the loss of his healthy life. But even worse than that was her overwhelming sense of frustration that she and Jim had wasted years and years worrying about the children, and their savings, and their jobs, and who should clean the bath, and which of them should pay the phone bill – and so on.

'I realise now that we were happy before Jim had his stroke, but I never saw it then, because I was always too busy worrying about silly things that really didn't matter at all,' she wrote.

To return to *you*, fortunately there's a high chance that you're going to live not only through today and tonight, but for very many years to come. Given reasonable luck, you're also going to enjoy good health – and hopefully your nearest and dearest will too.

So what are you going to do with this, your very precious life? Are you going to squander it by wallowing in woe, misery and envy? Or are you, from this moment on, going to get the happiness habit?

But *is* happiness a habit, you might ask? Isn't it a gift? Or a talent bestowed by God, or fate, to some people who were born luckier than the rest of us?

No. Happiness is not a gift or a talent – though it's true that some humans appear to have a more natural aptitude for it than others do. *Happiness is a skill, which, with practice, can turn into a habit.* In fact, showing happiness is the very first skill that we learn for ourselves.

When babies are born, they come already equipped to function in a number of ways. Barring accidents, they know how to breathe, sleep and cry. They also know how to suckle at one end and to eliminate waste products from the other. They may be contented – it's not always easy to tell – but we don't see any evidence of real, energetic happiness in our infants until they learn to smile, at around ten weeks. They then generally acquire the happiness habit very quickly, so long as they live in a loving environment.

The baby smiles, because he feels good. His smile makes Mum feel good. She smiles back. Baby gurgles with delight; his new-found joy reinforced by Mum's smiling face and attention. Thus a skill is acquired and a habit is formed.

You might compare the happiness habit with riding a bicycle. Do you remember becoming the proud owner of your first two-wheeler? If you were like me you feared you'd never master it, and you pleaded with your father not to let go as he steadied the bike while you tentatively perched on the saddle. And then, one day, your confidence took flight, and suddenly you rode away on your own, leaving poor old Dad panting behind you. You had learned to balance. You had learned a skill, and that skill became such an automatic habit that in the end you couldn't even remember the learning process and how difficult it had seemed.

Happiness is like that. It can become *your* habit, and when it does, life will never seem so difficult again. Of course I can't promise you that nothing sad, or inconvenient, or annoying, or even tragic will ever happen. What I can say, however, is that once you've learned the happiness habit, and trained yourself to grasp the happiness option at every opportunity, you will spend the greater part of your life in a state of contentment.

But hang on, you might say; it's one thing to accept that happiness is a skill that can become a habit, but how can it possibly be an option? Surely you either feel happy or you don't?

Not true. Of course a desperate and sudden crisis can only ever result in tears and immediate pain. But in very many situations, every single day, we actually have a second or two where we can select our emotion, instead of allowing it to select us.

Let's pretend, for example, that you lay in bed for an extra ten minutes this morning. Then, just as you were about to leave your flat, the telephone rang and you stopped to answer it. Very late now, you ran from the building, only to cut your finger badly on the broken gatepost you've been meaning to have fixed. Knowing that there were no sticking plasters in your home – even had you had time to return for one – you wrapped a scrappy looking tissue round your wound: this proved totally inadequate and, as you ran, you noticed that blood was dripping up your arm onto your new suit. It was raining hard and a car driving too close to the kerb drenched you with spray. Worst of all, when you reached the station, you saw your train pulling away without you.

You'd have to be a saint not to react with fury at this chain of events. If it had happened to me I'd certainly have uttered several rude expletives, and would expect you to do the same! But it's what might happen *next* that's important.

In that angry moment you would actually have a choice. You could either grasp the grumpy option – deciding that the whole day was ruined and that 'someone up there' never liked you and that life was endlessly unfair. Or you could breathe deeply and allow yourself a secret smile – a smile that would immediately lighten your mood and stop you from programming the next ten hours into an unremitting catastrophe.

So remember: *happiness is often a choice.* And the more you recognise those moments where there's a decision to be made about how you feel, the more accomplished you'll become at choosing happiness over misery.

Coming back to your Morning From Hell, let's pretend that you've finally reached your place of work and you've calmed down somewhat. Now is the time to re-think and rationalise what took place earlier.

You might be prepared to admit that you were responsible for getting up late. If you're feeling sensible, you might resolve to get more sleep tonight and to set your alarm to go off fifteen minutes earlier tomorrow. You could also make a decision that in future you'll let the answer-machine handle your morning calls, or that you'll simply let your phone ring. As for that gatepost, couldn't you get a friend, neighbour or local carpenter to fix it, if you can't do it yourself? And maybe you could buy a bumper pack of plasters? The rain – well, *that* you can do nothing about!

Now you can feel really virtuous. You had a bad start earlier, but you've overcome it. Not only that, you've taken full responsibility for the aspects of the situation that were within your control, and you've made several decisions to ensure that future mornings will run more smoothly. And you feel happier. Why? Because you've mentally chosen not to trot down the usual old cheerless cul-de-sac, but instead to laugh at yourself and to put right what you can. This is another important lesson: *happiness stems from being responsible and feeling in control.*

Unhappiness, on the other hand, stems from being *out* of control and *irresponsible*. What else do we know about it? Well, unhappiness, like happiness, is undeniably a choice – even though many people swear that they can't help being miserable. It's also a habit: a very bad habit, which can all too easily become addictive.

I'm going to confess now to having had the unhappiness habit myself in the past. When I was just twenty-two, I was teaching music in a comprehensive school. This was a stop-gap measure because what I really wanted to do was to be a professional singer.

I liked the actual teaching as it happens, but I was hopeless at all the routine, the pecking order and the discipline. And most of all, I was terrible at getting up in the morning. So I began each day determinedly miserable. I used to drive to school, swearing at other motorists, and by the time I arrived, I was fed up to the back teeth. Looking back, I can now see that I was constantly seeking out things to be angry and unhappy about.

My first daily duty as a music teacher was to play the piano for the morning assembly. Needless to say I hated this as well. So I used to arrive at the last moment and keep my coat on while I played: psychologically, I suppose I was pretending that I was just passing through and that the whole sorry business didn't have much to do with me! I used to keep my gloves on too – you try playing 'Dear Lord and Father of Mankind' wearing woolly mittens – which ensured that I made a hell of a mess of the hymn. Looking back, I'm sure my ungracious mood affected the other staff and the pupils and, quite rightly, I was ticked off several times by the deputy head. With hindsight it's easy to see that I was giving full rein to very childish emotions and that my misery was at least 95 per cent self-inflicted.

Still, it was quite a number of years before I grasped the fact that even while you're doing something you dislike, you can always find moments of pleasure in it. And that when you do find some peace or contentment in a situation you'd previously condemned as being dreadful, you lighten up and start enjoying life much more. Probably it's taken me all of the last thirty years to come to my current understanding of happiness – but then I didn't have the benefit of reading this book. You should do better!

Now let me tell you about Gordon. He's thirty-five, so he should have learned more sense. Gordon is a keen amateur tennis player, but he has one major problem. When he's decided to play, he treats any adverse weather conditions – and high winds in particular – as a personal insult. So he arrives at the court with pessimism oozing from every pore and remains doggedly miserable through three full sets.

This takes some doing, because exercising releases 'happy' chemicals in our brains. But Gordon resists any uplift in his mood, and after the match declares to anyone prepared to listen that he's had a dreadful time because he was put off by the wind. It never seems to occur to him that everyone else has been inconvenienced too. And it certainly never strikes him that he could use the inclement weather to play a different, more tactical kind of game. Not only that, he never smiles, nor does he allow himself to notice the birds singing; neither does his heart lift when the sun breaks through the clouds, nor does he ever stop to sniff the newly mown grass. Instead, he clings like a limpet to his unhappiness habit.

I'm sure you would agree that Gordon is wasting his leisure time – and that's very sad. Instead, with just a small shift of attitude, he could shrug off his disappointment by telling himself he was lucky it wasn't raining or snowing, when he wouldn't have been able to play at all. He could also go to the courts determined to enjoy himself, and he could plan ways to use the wind to outwit his opponents. In other words, he could choose the happiness option and work on his happiness habit – then he could go home a jollier and more satisfied fellow. But he doesn't.

People like Gordon can be found in every sports ground in the world. In fact, I'm sorry to say that there are far more miserable people – and miserable-looking people – around than happy ones. I can vouch for this because in the last few months, while I've been preparing this book, I've been keenly observing men and women of all ages throughout Europe. It's not a pretty sight! Their faces are set in grim expressions and their eyes rarely drag themselves away from the pavement. Also, their mouths appear taut and mean and their whole demeanour suggests that they have the world and its problems on their shoulders.

This kind of look is terribly ageing, which is as good a reason as any not to walk around looking glum all the time! In fact, it's almost impossible for anyone to look attractive and approachable when they're wallowing in melancholy.

I'm quite sure that some of the folk I've been watching have very real difficulties to contend with: they may be going through a marriage break-up, they may have a serious illness, or fear they are about to lose their jobs. But my guess is that the vast majority of them have simply got into the unhappiness habit – which is difficult, but not impossible, to break.

I can tell you now that even if you're locked into your own unhappiness habit, something very interesting will happen to you while you're reading this book. You'll become aware of the gloom in other people's faces and their apparent wretchedness. Not only that, you'll begin to resolve not to look like them, and not to look old before your time, and not to face the world with a grimace and dead-looking eyes.

You'll see a passenger on your bus with a thunderous expression, and your own features will immediately relax and lighten. You may not grin like a Cheshire cat. You may not even sense that you're feeling happier, but you will look it. And that's a very good start – because all sorts of positive improvements to your life and your mood will result. Cherish these changes, because they won't take much effort and they will prepare you for other shifts in your attitude that may prove more difficult.

Happiness is so very important and yet more and more people are claiming they don't have it. I know this to be a fact because I'm always being approached by individuals who think that I should be able to 'make' them happy. It's not always easy for them to under-stand that a psychotherapist, or a counsellor, or an agony aunt, or even an author of a book like this can only try to help. The stark truth is that *we all have to take responsibility for finding our own happiness.*

You've begun that task, however – and beginning is the hardest bit. I'm sure you won't give up now.

Meanwhile, I want to look at another type of situation where people feel unhappy but resist doing anything about it – and that is where they're obsessed with one bad aspect of their lives.

Maureen is a typical example. She claims: 'I can't ever be happy until I meet the man of my dreams.'

Now I very much hope that Maureen does achieve her ambition. But suppose she doesn't? What then? Is she going to refuse to find happiness in *any* moment of her life just because that one vital ingredient hasn't fallen into her lap? Sadly, there are lots of Maureens around, living their lives in a desultory kind of way. They're not happy, but they're not prepared to do the work that would alter their lot, so they just drift.

If I have one basic reason for writing this book, it is that I would like more and more people to find happiness. I would like them to seize every day and to enjoy as much of their time as possible. This is what I think of as energetic living. Sadly, vast numbers of indi-viduals soldier on with a policy of *non*-energetic living. They take the line of least resistance and don't see why they should bother to try harder. I suppose they want good fortune to flow down upon them, like golden rain, from the skies. But life isn't like that. You only get out of it what you put in. And people like Maureen, who believe they cannot feel happy until something happens – and who are waiting for something to change without any effort from them – are effectively cutting off their chances of happiness. More than that, they're putting their real lives on hold and existing on autopilot.

Let me tell you that years can race by when people get into this state. They become sadder and lazier with every succeeding month – and all because they're not prepared to think out their situation and put a bit more oomph into it.

So, I beg you, don't be a Maureen. Please accept that *this is your real life now! It's ticking away whether you like it or not. You are responsible for it, and you cannot put it 'on hold' just because you're feeling down.*

I'm not being unsympathetic; I do realise that your present circumstances may not be what you would have chosen. I also accept that you may feel that your existence is dull, uninteresting, unfair and unfulfilled, but I *don't* accept that you can do nothing about it. You cannot put your life away onto a shelf, and leave it there till some magical moment arrives to persuade you that it's worth dusting over and using again. Life continues, no matter what. It's not a dress rehearsal, and while we delay enjoying it – by waiting for the right job, the divorce, the pay rise, or the new love to arrive – it slips by with frightening speed.

I've lost count of the number of times I've received letters saying: 'I've been having a hopeless affair for seventeen years – why on earth didn't I see before that I was wasting my life?' Or: 'I was so obsessed with climbing the career ladder that I neglected my friends and family, and never had a baby. I wasn't ever happy, and now I realise that I've used up the best years of my life.'

Don't be like these correspondents. From today, start looking for enjoyment even in the bad or dull times. Doesn't it make more sense to live as actively as possible, instead of allowing time to pass you by?

This brings me to the next aspect of happiness that I want to share with you. If you appear happy, you'll bring happiness to other people, and you'll also receive happiness back from them.

Take Moira, who is a nurse. She works in a busy Accident and Emergency Department. She came to see me because she was thoroughly miserable with her life. She thought she wanted to go to university to study to be a doctor, but she had young children and felt she must keep her job till she had more money behind her. The job was hell, she told me. No one around her was happy either, which was very depressing. The other staff, like her, were overworked and underpaid, and the patients were often angry, because they had to wait so long to be seen.

Together we decided on an experiment where she would try extremely hard to increase her smiling-rate, no matter how dire her day might seem. Within weeks, the transformation in her working day astonished her. She said that smiling, even when she felt a bit artificial about it, caused her to feel more cheerful immediately.

But the real bonus was that all the staff and patients appeared to like her better. They started smiling back at her and their new warmth meant that she valued herself more. In addition, she began to enjoy her job and to feel more energised by it, where before it had left her utterly drained. She became known as 'Smiler' and loved the fact that she had a definite identity in the department. And she enjoyed telling me that the A&E department was a jollier place now where people laughed and joked more than they had previously.

'It was an effort at first,' she said to me at our last meeting. 'But it was well worth it. I now feel content most of the time and I look forward to work rather than dreading it. I also feel in a better position to make a decision about my long-term career, simply because I'm happier and seeing things more clearly.'

Watching the change in Moira, over a few weeks, was very rewarding for me. I know she has important choices to make and that she may spend a lot of time yet being exhausted and having little money, but I feel confident she's on the right path, because her mood has lifted to the point where she is embracing life rather than avoiding it.

Recently, I was travelling on a London underground train – not my favourite pastime generally – and I was able to witness an absolutely classic example of how happiness in one individual can lift the mood of countless others.

A child of two was travelling on this same train, with her mum. She was a cute and very engaging little soul and so infectiously happy that everyone who came into that carriage caught her eye and started smiling and laughing.

I watched carefully as buttoned-up city gents in pinstriped suits played peekaboo with her from behind the financial pages of their newspapers. Students pulled funny faces at her. Career women relaxed their tense expressions into beaming smiles. And school children, instead of quarrelling among themselves, chatted to her and vied with each other for her attention.

This was one of the most compelling illustrations of the power of happiness that I've ever seen. I know that everyone who was in that compartment that day was elevated by the contact with that little girl. Sheer energetic joy poured out of her and I'm convinced that even at the age of two, she sensed the power it gave her. I can only hope that she never loses her happiness habit.

Before I come to the end of this introductory chapter, I want to tell you about one of my ex-clients. I shall call her Katie, but needless to say that's not her name and I've altered certain details of her case to protect her anonymity.

I came to know Katie very well over a period of more than six months. I don't mind admitting now that when she first arrived in my consulting room I found her extremely difficult, inconsistent and awfully wearing.

She was a bright and attractive woman in her early thirties, and she had sought me out because she felt very unhappy and 'stuck'. She also had a difficult relationship with her parents.

It turned out that Katie had an interesting but poorly paid job in publishing where she worked absurdly long hours. One of her gripes was that the company was full of women, so she never had the opportunity to mix with men. And – she whined – she was unlikely to meet any men outside work, because her long hours were so exhausting that she never went anywhere and never had time to socialise. She was overstressed, fatigued, tearful and alone; apparently there had been boyfriends in the past, but they had tended to be self-centred – if fascinating – and they had all let her down.

She frequently said: 'Everything happens to me.' And when I tried, very gently, to suggest that her happiness was ultimately her own responsibility, she was not impressed with the concept.

Meanwhile, if anything could go wrong for Katie it did, and it was always 'unfair'. When she wanted to go anywhere, trains always ran late, or were cancelled. When she needed to call someone to say that she was late because of the trains, phones were always out of order. If she was driving, other cars would leap out and crash into her, but this was never her fault. She was invariably late for our sessions and sometimes forgot to come at all.

She hardly needed to tell me that she irritated her colleagues, because she irritated the hell out of me. It's very common, by the way, for a client to evoke the same feelings in her therapist as she does in her workmates, friends and family.

I kept trying to get the therapy back on track, but it was a struggle. Several times Katie asked me, rather tearfully, if I wanted to give up on her. But I refused to do it. I believed she could change and I wanted more than anything for her to believe this too.

Meanwhile she was often very, very unhappy and I did feel considerable admiration for her that she never took time off from her job even when she was feeling like death. But though it was important to offer her unconditional acceptance and support – and a certain amount of sympathy – this alone could never be enough. She had to take charge of her life – and only she could do that.

I was quite tough with her. I encouraged her to write down a plan of her day, every day, and to try to stick to it. I nagged her into bringing more order into her life. I also tried to train her to leave more time for travelling when she was going to work, or seeing me. At first, she thought it a crazy idea to leave home a full thirty minutes earlier than usual, but gradually she came to like the feeling of being not just on time, but *early*.

Piece by piece, we worked on removing the unhappiness and the stress in her life that it was within her power to alter.

The summer holidays were approaching. She always took three weeks' vacation, but in the past had generally used the time to go somewhere with her parents. She had an overbearing father who terrified her, and an emotionally clinging mother who exhausted her, so holidaying with them could never be a bundle of laughs. Worse than that, in Katie's everyday working life, her mother and father seemed to be far too much of a presence for comfort. In fact they had been known to ring her at work and put her in such a tizz that she made noticeable and expensive mistakes.

Together we worked out a means of dealing with them. This involved announcing to them that private calls at work had been banned. Katie then bought an answer-machine, which meant that she could limit contact with her very exacting parents to just two conversations per week at home. This act alone brought tremendous relief to my client and she found that stopping the daily and often upsetting calls to and from her parents gave her more space to breathe.

We then tackled the holidays, agreeing on a compromise whereby she would spend one week with her parents, and then take herself off on a walking trip with a girlfriend. Breaking this news to her family took enormous courage, but Katie was on cloud nine after achieving it.

Each week as she dealt with more and more problems, and persevered with structuring and controlling her life, her spirits rose. She began to sleep better. She found she was more organised at work and therefore didn't need to spend so much time at the office. And every time I saw her it seemed to me that she became more peaceful, more poised, more content and really more physically lovely. Admittedly, she had always taken great care with her clothes, but now her whole demeanour changed from that of a hard-done-by, frustrated, rather hysterical woman, into a softer, contented one with relaxed, attractive features and shining eyes.

I was overjoyed that Katie did the work necessary to take control of her life and her emotions – especially because our early sessions had been so fraught.

Of course there was one particular aspect of her original present-ing problem that we hadn't actually tackled. We hadn't found her the right man. But I never promise anyone that, and Katie knew it.

I do have a theory, however, which I tell my clients, and it is this. When people take charge of themselves and their happiness, and sort out as much of their lives as they can, and learn to value themselves more, then, very frequently, romance rears its rosy head. It happens time and time again.

We were nearing the end of Katie's treatment – and she knew I was enormously pleased with her, and proud of her too. Then, one day, she announced rather shyly that she had met 'someone'.

It transpired that she had been to a book launch at her firm and had met a quiet, clever man who was an accountant. She wasn't sure where this relationship might lead, but he did seem very keen on her and, like her, he was interested in the theatre and reading and walking.

'But he's not at all the type I would normally go for,' she said anxiously.

'Good thing too,' I said, remembering the string of disastrous men who had let her down. She giggled – and she looked happy and young and carefree.

'But I don't want to be the sort of woman who's happy just because there's a man in tow,' she said, suddenly serious.

'Katie,' I laughed, 'he's only come into your life *because* you're happy.' And I'm sure that was the truth. Katie had worked very hard to control her life and to take responsibility for it. She was no longer the stressed, chaotic woman who thought that 'everything happens to me'.

Last time I saw her, the romance was going well. I told her that she deserved it. She looked at me for a long moment, and then she smiled the warm, easy smile that was becoming an automatic part of her. 'I guess perhaps I do,' she said quietly.

Most of the methods I used with Katie have found their way into this book. She worked hard – and developed a happiness habit. You can do it too.

Chapter One Key Points:
The Ten Happiness Facts

- Happiness is something we can all work at.
- Happiness is a skill.
- Happiness can become a habit.
- Happiness is often a choice.
- Happiness stems from feeling in charge of our lives.
- We are all responsible for finding our own happiness.
- If you put your life on hold hoping that happiness will simply happen – you might wait for ever.
- Happiness is infectious.
- Happiness makes you look younger.
- Happiness makes you more attractive.

2

The Happiness Quiz

Most of us secretly enjoy filling in quizzes, whether they're about our love lives, our money, or what sort of holidays suit us best. So here's a happiness quiz for you.

I've already tried it out on many clients and friends, and the results have been very illuminating – mostly, I suspect, because the questions cover so many aspects of our lives.

By completing the quiz you'll not only gain a better idea of how happy, or unhappy, you are, but you'll also discover which areas in your life are most problematic.

So have a go at it now and see how you get on. May I then suggest that once you've finished the book you tackle it again – when you should see a significant improvement in your levels of happiness. In fact, you might like to think of this quiz – at any time in your life – as a useful monitor of your contentment. So that if you ever fear your happiness habit is slipping, you can go through the questions again and quickly establish where your troubles lie.

Some small parts of the quiz may not apply to you. For example, you may not have children or siblings, while another person reading this book probably has both. But just answer all the questions that you can by ticking one of the three options: never, sometimes or often.

Figure 1: The Happiness Quiz

Section (a) GENERAL MOODS:	NEVER	SOMETIMES	OFTEN
1 Do you feel miserable?			
2 Do you feel that life is passing you by?			
3 Do you feel that life is unfair?			
4 Do you feel that life is too much effort?			
5 Do you feel numb – neither happy nor unhappy?			
6 Do you feel a sense of hopelessness?			
7 Do you ever feel that everyone would be better off if you were dead?			
8 Do you think about killing yourself?			
9 Do you find it difficult to experience joy in little things like a bird singing, or a child's smile?			
10 Does bad weather make you feel sadder?			
11 Do you worry that you might become seriously mentally ill?			
12 Do you spend long periods of time totally alone?			
13 Do you prefer communicating with others on the Internet, rather than by phone or in person?			
14 Do you find decision-making very difficult?			
15 Do you find yourself dwelling on violent or morbid thoughts – like being murdered, or injured in a crash?			

	NEVER	SOMETIMES	OFTEN

Section (b) STRESS:

1 Do you feel that your life is chaotic?

2 Do you feel 'out of control'?

3 Do you have a sense that you're running constantly without ever catching up?

4 Do you feel that bad things keep 'happening' to you through no fault of your own?

5 Do you keep promising yourself that you'll get organised – but just don't get round to it?

6 Do you feel insecure if things aren't neat?

7 Do you ever have panic attacks?

8 Do you ever feel breathless, tingly or sweaty?

9 Are you ever aware of your heart beating fast?

10 Do you ever feel like a 'coiled spring' or as if you could burst with tension?

11 Is it hard for you to feel satisfaction, even when things go well?

12 Are you bored?

13 Do you find concentrating difficult?

14 Do you feel you haven't enough to do?

15 Do you feel stuck in a rut?

16 Do you feel irritable?

17 Do you find it hard to control your anger?

18 Do you feel tearful when confronted with problems?

Section (c) SELF-ESTEEM:

1 Do you dislike yourself?

2 Is it hard for you to love yourself?

3 Do you feel that other people dislike you?

4 Do you feel that your opinion doesn't matter?

5 Do you find it difficult to express yourself in company?

	NEVER	SOMETIMES	OFTEN

6 Do you think you are inadequate compared with others?

7 Would your feelings about yourself stop you from seeking promotion?

8 Do you feel you must always be a follower rather than a leader?

9 Are you shy?

10 Are you lacking in confidence?

11 Do you believe you can't be happy if you're not in a relationship?

Section (d) DIET, HEALTH AND LOOKS:

1 Do you feel you look older than you are?

2 Do you dislike your looks?

3 Do you feel that changing how you look would be impossible, or too much bother?

4 Is your diet very unbalanced?

5 Do you fill up on foods you know are bad for you?

6 Do you find it difficult to get interested in food?

7 Do you have anxieties about eating?

8 Do you starve yourself, or binge, or both?

9 Do you drink more than 14 units of alcohol per week if you're a woman – or over 21 units per week if you're a man?

10 Do you feel nervous if you can't get a drink when you want?

11 Do you drink to escape your stress or unhappiness?

12 Do you ever get seriously drunk?

13 Do you smoke?

14 Do you smoke more than 20 a day?

15 Do you prefer smoking or drinking to buying nice food for yourself and eating it?

	NEVER	SOMETIMES	OFTEN
16 Do you worry about your health?			
17 Do you suffer from odd aches or funny feelings?			
18 Do you feel you're never quite fit and well?			
19 Do you take more time off work than other colleagues?			
20 Do you sleep badly?			
21 Do you go off to sleep OK, but wake in the early morning and find it hard to sleep again?			
22 Do you sleep too much?			
23 Do you feel exhausted?			
24 Do you exercise for less than twenty minutes a day, three days a week?			

Section (e) RELATIONSHIPS:

	NEVER	SOMETIMES	OFTEN
1 If you're in a relationship, are you unhappy in it?			
2 Do you worry that your partner might leave you?			
3 Are you surprised that your partner stays with you?			
4 Do you feel that your relationship is going nowhere?			
5 Even when you know you're in a bad relationship, do you find it terribly difficult to leave it?			
6 Is your partner unkind to you?			
7 Is your partner ever violent towards you?			
8 Do you feel that most people's relationships must be better than yours?			
9 Do you feel it's unlikely that you'll ever have a really lovely, romantic, happy and permanent relationship?			
10 Do you feel a lack of interest in your current relationship?			

	NEVER	SOMETIMES	OFTEN
11 Do you feel you've lost interest in having *any* relationship?			

Section (f) SEX:

	NEVER	SOMETIMES	OFTEN
1 Does sex tend to be unsatisfying or disappointing?			
2 Do you feel you've gone off sex?			
3 Do you have problems with climaxing?			
4 Have you stopped even thinking about sex?			
5 Do you feel that your sex life is in a rut?			
6 Do you feel you don't get enough love and cuddling?			
7 Do you use sex to get power, or in an attempt to make people like or love you?			
8 Do you sacrifice sex so that you can sleep more?			
9 Does sex seem like too much effort?			
10 Do you fake orgasm?			
11 If you've been raped, does this past event cause problems in your sex life now?			
12 If you've had a background of childhood sexual abuse, do you feel that this has ruined your sex life?			

Section (g) JOB:

	NEVER	SOMETIMES	OFTEN
1 Are you unhappy at work?			
2 Does your job exhaust you?			
3 Do you feel that work takes up too much of your time?			
4 Do you feel that your firm and employers should be more aware that you need a family-life and free time?			
5 If you're freelance, or a home-worker, do you find it difficult to keep enough time for your private life?			
6 Is your job frustrating?			

	NEVER	SOMETIMES	OFTEN
7 Is your boss a pain?			
8 Do you feel that your colleagues get on with people better than you do?			
9 Do you feel unappreciated?			
10 Do you feel underpaid?			
11 Is it hard for you to say 'no'?			
12 Even if you dislike a job, do you find it difficult to give it up or look for another?			

Section (h) YOUR VALUES

	NEVER	SOMETIMES	OFTEN
1 Do you feel that your values are very different from those of your parents?			
2 Are you unhappy with your current set of values?			
3 Do you feel you've become mean-spirited?			
4 Are you selfish?			
5 Have you decided that because you're going through such a bad patch, you can't spare time or money to help anyone else?			
6 Do you feel bitter that people don't help you more?			
7 Do you feel that problems like the homeless are nothing to do with you?			
8 Do you resent being asked for money for charity?			
9 Do you think that generous people are just mugs?			
10 Would you avoid paying a fare if you thought you could get away with it?			
11 If you found a wallet full of money in the street, would you keep it rather than hand it in to the police?			
12 Do you think you should always put yourself first – because that's the way of the world?			

	NEVER	SOMETIMES	OFTEN

Section (i) INNER LIFE:

1 Do you avoid thinking about religion?
2 Do you think that life's too tough and busy for you to worry about things like spirituality?
3 Do you remain unmoved by 'great' music?
4 Do you wonder what all the fuss is about when someone gets lyrical over a sunset?
5 Do you think that poetry is for wimps?

Section (j) FAMILY

1 If you're a parent, do you seriously wish that you'd never had children?
2 Do you feel that having children has ruined your current relationship?
3 Even though you're an adult, do you feel jealous about the attention your brothers and sisters get from your parents?
4 Do you feel that your father never loved you enough?
5 Do you feel that your mother never loved you enough?
6 Do you feel that your parents are the root cause of your current problems?
7 Do you find it difficult to feel close to any of your family?
8 Do you feel so close to your family, that no one else can begin to compare with them?
9 Does thinking about family issues like these make you feel especially tearful?

Section (k) INTERESTS:

1 Do you feel that your interests and hobbies just aren't very important?

23

	NEVER	SOMETIMES	OFTEN

2 Have you lost enthusiasm for most of your usual interests?

3 Do you use your hobbies to fill your time so you can avoid people?

4 Are you reluctant to take up new interests because you don't think you'll cope with them?

5 Do you sometimes catch yourself enjoying an activity, but then deliberately stop your enjoyment because there's no place for nice feelings in your overall misery?

Section (l) FRIENDS:

1 Do you find it hard to lean on your friends?

2 Do you avoid your friends?

3 Do you feel that other people have far more friends than you do?

4 Does it seem that your friends rarely contact you, and that if you want to meet them, you're the one who has to organise it?

5 Do you feel that your friends are bored by you and your problems?

6 Do you feel that you don't have *any* very close friends?

7 Do you find it difficult to make friends?

8 Do you feel that making friends is quite easy, but holding on to them is the difficult bit?

Section (m) THE FUTURE:

1 Does the future look hopeless?

2 Do you believe that life can never get any better?

3 Do you dread birthdays?

4 Do you dread Christmas?

	NEVER	SOMETIMES	OFTEN
5 Do you dread New Year?			
6 Do you feel it's better not to anticipate any happiness, because then you need never feel any more disappointment?			
7 Do you feel that fate has ordained you should have a miserable life, so it's not worth trying to change it?			
8 Do you feel there is a possibility that life may improve, but that all you can do is wait for it to happen?			

Now that you've completed the quiz, I suggest you take a rest and have a cup of tea – or something stronger! These questions take time and effort to answer, and they probe your most private thoughts, so don't worry if you're now a bit tired and emotional.

You might even want to pause in your reading of the book for a few days while you come to terms with any feelings that have come to the fore while doing the quiz. Sometimes people are quite shocked by the way they have answered certain questions. If this applies to you, please don't worry, just take your time and come back to the next part of this chapter when you can.

OK – once you're ready, I want you to do one thing before we go on to look at your responses. I'd like you to glance back to the end of Chapter One and to look again at The Ten Happiness Facts. In fact, if you can memorise them, that will be even better. Chapter One was all about absorbing new ideas, but as we go through Chapter Two, I'm going to give you a number of tasks to do, so you'll become much more active in helping yourself to get the happiness habit. These tasks will be easier if you've got your Ten Happiness Facts at your fingertips.

Now, what do your quiz answers actually mean? The first thing to take on board is that there are no right or wrong answers. But I'm sure you've realised by now that the 'often' answers show the areas in your life where you're miserable, stressed and dissatisfied, while the 'never' answers indicate where you're quite happy, safe and secure.

So, are you normal in your levels of happiness? Or are you better, or worse than that? Well, to give you some kind of yardstick, I'm going to tell you how three very different people filled in the quiz.

I was the first guinea pig! And before I declare my answers, I must tell you that nowadays I am a deeply contented person. But that wasn't always so. At different times, I've had spells of desperate unhappiness. One of the worst was in my teens. Then, in my mid-thirties, when I had a successful, well-paid media career – and appeared to have more going for me than most folk – I hit a wall of depression that lasted several years. In fact, had I been asked to complete my own quiz in about 1984, I'd have ticked 'often' to virtually every question!

But how did I answer today? Well, I only ticked the 'often' column three times. However, I'm not complacent about that score. I can see that a couple of my 'oftens' show up problems that I probably need to sort.

I do have a fair sprinkling of 'sometimes' ticks, but the vast majority of my ticks – about ninety-five of them – went into the 'never' column. So, though I know I can still improve in some areas, I can safely say that I'm a walking advert for my own theory that people – and this includes you – can turn their lives around and find the happiness habit!

Forty-two-year-old Andrew also filled in the quiz. He is a dentist with a wife and family. He appears to be a fairly contented person, but he's a terrible worrier. His quiz answers are as follows: he has over thirty 'oftens', about forty 'sometimes' ticks and around seventy 'nevers'.

He's jolly pleased about one thing, which is that he has almost a clean sweep of 'nevers' in the Sex and Relationship sections, so his love life is clearly in buoyant shape! Andrew always puts his wife and family before his ambition, so he's delighted to see that reflected in the quiz.

But Andrew has far too many 'oftens' in the General Moods section, and also in the one on Diet, Health and Looks. So his result shows that though he is relatively contented, he still has many areas of unhappiness which he needs to put right.

Now I'll tell you about twenty-seven-year-old Melinda. She is one of my clients who is finding life extremely tough. She is desperately miserable and her sadness is preventing her from getting motivated to do anything. In fact, she's so convinced that she's condemned to be lonely and depressed that she heavily resists most of my efforts to get her to look at her life from other, more positive, angles. I know this will pass, but right now she doesn't believe anything can change, and she's having a really rotten time. Her results reflect the mood she's stuck in.

Melinda has clocked up a large total of 'oftens', which is, of course, what one might expect. But there's a glimmer of hope: unlike Andrew, she scores surprisingly well in the Diet, Health and Looks section.

Her answers in that section will be very helpful in my future work with her, and I'll tell you why. Through the years I've discovered that once sad people finally accept that there are some happy areas in their lives, they always start finding others.

In fact, the pursuit of happiness is pretty much like tackling a giant jigsaw – the kind that families buy to keep themselves busy all through Christmas, where you need a huge dining table and loads of patience! Have you ever tried one? If you have, you'll know that you go through different phases while you wrestle with it. You feel enthusiastic, but then you get annoyed, or tired, or dispirited. But somehow, once you've got your corner pieces in place – and then a few of the side pieces – you get hooked and you keep coming back to it, trying to find places for all sorts of fiddly little bits until the picture makes sense and is finally complete.

Building happiness is just like that. Get some pieces in place and others will follow. This is something I want you to think about as we go through this chapter.

Now, your quiz answers may be like mine, or like Andrew's, or maybe you're at the end of your tether like Melinda. But by reading this book, you're demonstrating your desire to become a happier person, and I want to help to achieve your goal as quickly as possible. So what we'll do now is to look at your quiz answers as a whole.

Like Andrew, you've probably got some sections of the quiz that you're very pleased with. But you've almost certainly got other sections packed with 'oftens'. Look at these 'often' sections for a moment: these are the areas of your life that you really need to work on. And to begin that work, I want you to ask yourself the following two questions about these particular answers:

• Are you worrying over factors beyond your control?
• Are you allowing yourself to wallow in misery when you could sometimes select a happier mood?

You probably won't be able to answer these questions immediately, but just keep coming back to them. By opening your mind to the possibility that you may be exaggerating your unhappiness rather than seeking the happiness option, you'll gradually begin to assess your life and your moods differently. In other words, your mind-set will become *less* set and you'll let go of old, irrational and unhelpful beliefs that have sustained your past misery.

Now I'm going to take you through the quiz – section by section:

Section (a) General moods

This first section is about how you feel and how you appear to other people. And if you've answered 'often' to a number of questions in this section, then you're not only fed up, but you're also presenting a very downbeat image of yourself to your colleagues, your friends and your family.

In fact, if you have answered 'often' to questions 7, 8 and 15, you may need a bit more help than I alone can give you. Your answers indicate that you're very 'low' and you may be clinically depressed, so though I remain confident that this book can change your life for the better, I'd also like you to see your GP in case he or she feels you need additional medical support.

However, the vast majority of people are not ill, they simply need to learn how to get more happiness out of life. And that's where this book comes in.

You see, if you apply the Ten Happiness Facts from Chapter One to your answers in this General Moods section, you'll find that you'll gradually stop answering 'often' to so many questions.

For a start, you can *choose* to find happiness in many of life's miserable moments. It takes practice, but you can do it. You can also stop putting your life on hold and resolve to live it more fully and actively, even when your present circumstances are unpleasant.

In addition, you can look out for happy moments when they occur, and learn to recognise and cherish them. For example, you can train yourself to notice a bird singing, or a sudden shaft of sunlight, or a raindrop trembling on a new crocus.

In fact, I'm now going to set you a task of spotting *five* heart-gladdening sights or sounds every day. This may feel like very hard work at first, but you'll be amazed at how much extra joy it will bring you. And as your happiness habit becomes stronger and more reliable, you'll find that you notice more and more pleasurable moments all the time.

More than that, as your mood lifts and you find more happiness in your day-to-day living, other people will reflect these good feelings back to you. You see, when you appear happy, pleasant and approachable, other people treat you in a more friendly and open way. Do you remember Moira, my nurse client in Chapter One? By presenting a happier front she *became* happier. Then she had lots of positive feedback from her colleagues and friends, which cheered her up even more!

I'm not asking you to live a lie; all I want you to do is to put a happy spin on feelings or events wherever you can.

I wonder what you answered to question 10 about bad weather? I'd say that it's entirely natural to feel happier when the sun is shining – I certainly do. But you *don't* have to allow inclement conditions to ruin your day. You can choose to say to yourself: 'I wish it were brighter – or not raining – but I won't get upset over something I cannot change.'

If you answered 'often' to question 13 about the Internet, this is something that you *can* change. You have freedom of will, so use it. I'm sure you don't need me to tell you that if you find meeting, mixing and mingling a nightmare, you won't improve your 'people' skills by tapping away at your computer. Admittedly the Internet is one way of making contact with others, but if you do it to the exclusion of face-to-face social intercourse – or any other sort of intercourse for that matter – you'll become a total nerd!

As I've already said, this first section is about feelings – feelings that are often really horrid – but just remember that you can re-educate your mind to look for pleasure, even in pain, and you can train yourself to get the happiness habit.

The last point I want to make about the first section is that many people who are tired, unhappy and stressed, fear that they might become seriously mentally ill. Many of us have had, or will need to have, treatment for depression or anxiety at some time in our lives, but I want to reassure you that most people who worry about becoming *seriously* ill, or 'going mad', never do. However, if you want further reassurance about this, please do see your own doctor.

Section (b) Stress

Let's look now at the Stress Section of your quiz. So many people feel badly stressed these days that I've devoted the whole of Chapter Five to the subject.

Although stress isn't the same thing as misery by any means – and you can feel quite high on it sometimes – persistent stress and tension make people feel that their lives are in chaos. And when people feel that their lives are chaotic, they generally also feel hopeless and unhappy. But I can promise you that if you're downcast because your life feels out of control, you *can* change your life for the better. You can get organised. And when you feel yourself to be more in command and more relaxed, you will inevitably experience an uplift in mood – just as Katie did in Chapter One.

Stress is the most overworked word in the modern world – and some of it you simply have to learn to live with. For example, it's not your fault that your day-to-day existence is about a hundred times noisier than that of your eighteenth-century ancestors. But you can't turn that particular clock back unless you opt out to go and live in the remotest part of the Scottish Highlands!

Commuting is another terrible strain for many of us. But you may be simply unable to avoid it for the time being. Similarly, you may wish that your employer issued long-term contracts instead of short-term ones, but you may have to accept that you alone can't change their system.

So what *can* you do? Well, you can learn to limit the damage of the resulting tension, by structuring your life into better shape and balance, and by finding as much calm in your situation as the madness of the twenty-first century will allow.

I want you to start this right now with the Ten-Minute Soother. I told you I'd be working you hard in this chapter – but this is a very pleasant task indeed. All you have to do is to find ten minutes a day when you can sit down quietly and talk to no one. You shouldn't read, or eat, or worry, or watch television during these ten minutes. All you're required to do is to be quietly alone, and to let your mind wander over pleasant memories of places or things.

Believe me, no matter how stressed out you feel, you can find ten minutes a day. When people tell me that they *can't*, I know they're telling me they *won't* – which is not the same thing at all. People who won't find time for this soothing exercise are resisting the chance to change and to acquire the happiness habit. Don't let that be you.

The Ten-Minute Soother will help with all sorts of the problems you may have highlighted in the quiz's stress section. It will help you to feel more in control – as well as calm your heart rate, stop you feeling breathless and keep your tears at bay. It will also clear your mind and aid your concentration. And best of all, it will rid you of that awful 'coiled spring' sensation that is so distressing.

Section (c) Self-esteem

Self-esteem is *crucial* to happiness, but it's a quality that miserable people often find hard to acquire. So, if you scored very poorly in this section, just remember that learning to appreciate yourself is a joyful discovery that you can begin today and continue throughout your life.

Despite your most punishing thoughts, you are lovable and unique. So start thinking about your special qualities and talents. You certainly have some, and you can learn to value them – and yourself.

Of course a lack of self-esteem shows up in all sorts of areas of our lives – and if this is one of your problems, you should also pay special attention to the later quiz sections on relationships, sex and jobs.

But in this section of the quiz I'm concentrating on your self-worth, your confidence and your shyness.

You'll have noticed that there are only eleven questions. If you've answered 'often' to five or more of them, then your self-esteem is crying out for attention.

There may be many reasons for this – some of which you'll uncover as you continue to read the book – but I want you to improve how you feel about yourself, starting right now. So here's a task that will get you thinking more positively about yourself.

I want you to smile and say 'hello' to three different strangers every day. You can do it. I know it'll seem an ordeal at first, but gradually it will become automatic.

When you select your people each day, I want you to feel that you're giving them a special gift by greeting them. And I want you to tell yourself that these folk are jolly lucky you've honoured them with your attention. Try to feel a bit like the Queen, or a famous actress, and then enjoy the pleasure that you're bringing to these strangers by speaking to them.

Lastly in this section, let me tell you something that is very important: people who are real no-hopers in life don't go out and buy, or borrow, books like mine. They don't – because they refuse to commit to anything this positive. So just by reading this book, you're showing that you care for yourself and that you're working towards your happiness habit. And if you also tackle all the tasks I give you, then you'll really be grasping the reins of responsibility for a vastly improved life.

Section (d) Diet, health and looks

This section is all about how you perceive yourself – and whether or not you're taking care of you, the most special person in the world.

When you're miserable, bothering with your appearance and your health can just seem one step too far: you may also be going through a phase of hating how you look.

But let me just remind you that one of the Ten Happiness Facts tells us that happiness makes us look younger. Well, this is undeniably true, so as you pursue the happiness habit, I can confidently predict that the years will roll off you – all without the aid of plastic surgery!

Unfortunately, one of the main troubles with unhappy people is that they can't seem to find the energy to improve things, and it's easier by far to lapse into bad health habits.

When a new client comes to me and I establish that she's very miserable, I always ask her about eating properly and about exercising and whether she smokes or drinks too much. It's quite common for her to be doing everything wrong! Then she usually sighs deeply and I can actually see her thinking three little words: 'What the hell!' At that point the tears often flow – quiet, hopeless, dejected, heavy tears that are agony for the client to cry, and extraordinarily painful to watch.

It is such misery for people when they've reached the 'what-the-hell' stage. I've nursed many a client through it. I've also been there myself.

'What the hell!' I'd cry when I arrived home from work and poured myself a large drink before I'd even closed the front door, or taken my coat off.

'What the hell,' I'd mutter, as I reached for my twentieth cigarette of the evening.

'What the hell,' I'd murmur, as I wolfed down chips and chocolate at midnight, because I hadn't eaten all day.

'What the hell!' I'd yell to my office walls when I decided that yet again I had no time to go to the gym.

So I can spot someone who's not caring for themselves a mile off, because I used to be that person.

Of course you may say – as some of my patients do – that you need all these 'crutches' and that you'll find it much easier to give up bad habits when you're happier. I understand this theory, and I certainly sympathise with it: let's face it, it might not be the greatest idea to give up smoking the week your husband dumps you.

But I must tell you that all these factors that damage our health *don't* make us happier, or more stress-free. In fact, they contribute to our feelings of self-loathing, and they injure our health so that we actually feel physically ill as well as fed up. So the more you can do to eradicate your 'what the hell' attitude, and to cultivate one that responsibly cares for yourself, the better.

With my very unhappy patients, I ask them to tackle little changes. I don't demand that they use the gym twice weekly; instead I encourage them to get off the bus two stops early on their way to work and to walk that small extra distance. I don't insist that they stop drinking or smoking, but I do ask them to eat several pieces of fruit a day. Often by starting small, people begin to feel considerably better – both mentally and physically – and to accept that they're worth looking after.

So if you're treating yourself badly, try adding five pieces of fruit a day to your diet and also building some small amount of exercise into your routine: you will feel better for it.

Now, you'll have noticed in this section that there are questions about eating disorders. Problems around food often disappear when people feel generally happier and start liking themselves more. But this is not a book specifically tailored to anorexia or bulimia sufferers, or compulsive eaters either, and you might need more expert help than I can offer here. To get you on the right road, you'll find some useful addresses, and details of self-help manuals, in the directory at the end of the book.

One last thought before we leave the Diet, Health and Looks Section: you'll remember that one of the Ten Happiness Facts states you cannot put your life on hold until happiness miraculously happens. Well, nowhere is this truer than in regard to health. Sometimes, when people don't grasp this fact, they simply run out of time.

I can think of two male colleagues whose attitudes were so negative that they would certainly have sneered at the idea of reading a book like this. Both of them drank far too much and they each lived in a very 'what-the-hell' kind of way. Maybe they inwardly believed that one day they would clean up their acts. Well, they never got round to it as both of them died young.

Section (e) Relationships

This section will show you where your anxieties and your unhappiness lie in your current relationship – if you have one. And if you've answered 'often' to question 11, then you're obviously very fed up and disillusioned with relationships in general.

Most people believe that being in a good relationship is an essential part of being happy. Well, it can help – no doubt about that. But true contentment is *not* dependent on being in a relationship. In fact, if we believe we can't be happy without one, we're really saying that we don't place a high enough value on ourselves.

We have to find an inner core of contentment, which we're responsible for. If we look to someone else to make us happy, we're *always* going to end up disappointed.

Remember Katie in Chapter One: she worked hard at finding order and happiness and inner peace. And at the very point where she liked and valued herself and was content with her lot, a special person walked into her life.

But Katie had learned that she is responsible for her own happiness. So her new love is the well-earned icing – not the whole cake!

By the way, far too many of my clients have found love – once they've got their heads straight and their lives in order – for it to be a coincidence. When people gain confidence, happiness and poise they inevitably attract partners who would never have looked at them before. So that's another good reason for sorting yourself out!

If you answered 'often' to question 5 about finding it difficult to leave a bad relationship, your problem is more to do with self-esteem than anything. You need to do everything you can to boost it. Once you have, you'll see things differently and you won't put up with situations you might tolerate now.

Questions 6 and 7 are about verbally violent or physically abusive relationships. People in such situations are often so miserable and downcast that they cannot see any alternative but to stay in them. But there is *always* an alternative. This book will open your eyes to your own importance. But right now I beg you to take a look at the useful phone lines and organisations in the directory at the end of this book. You can reach out and find help immediately, if only you'll pick up the phone.

Maybe, as many people do, you've bought this book when you've just emerged from a long-term relationship, which has ended through rejection, or death or divorce. These are very painful times for you, but you will recover, and there is no reason at all why you should not build a fresh and happy life for yourself. It won't be the same of course, but it can be good – and you can do it.

What often holds people back is an irrational fear that though they have been loved, it can absolutely never happen again. Let me give you an example.

Gilly, a thirty-seven-year-old florist, came to see me. She was devastated because her husband had walked out, leaving her to run their business on her own, and to bring up their two sons.

Obviously she felt hugely rejected and angry and depressed; in fact there were so many emotions swilling around it was difficult to keep track of them.

'I'm so unhappy,' she whispered to me at our first session.

I nodded.

'And I feel so sad that my husband has left me,' she went on.

I nodded again.

'And no one else will ever want me again, and I'll be on my own for ever, and my whole life will be hateful,' she cried.

'Stop right there,' I said.

I then agreed with her about her sadness and how it was entirely justifiable. But I refused to go along with her subsequent irrational thoughts, because they weren't logical and they certainly weren't helping.

'You are sad, that's true,' I said. 'But you can't possibly *know* that nobody else will ever want you again.'

'But . . .' she began.

'No, let me finish,' I insisted. 'You can't possibly *know* that nobody else will ever want you. That is an irrational and illogical statement – and you're far too intelligent to believe it.'

'But I feel so awful,' she wailed, as tears flooded down her cheeks.

'I can see – and feel – that you do,' I said. 'There's no doubt about it. But that's not the same thing as "knowing" that nobody else will ever want you, or that you'll be on your own for ever, or that your life will always be hateful. You can't possibly know those things, so you're carrying around a bigger burden than you need. D'you see? You're suffering a whole load of stuff that almost certainly will never, ever happen.'

Gilly stopped crying and looked at me. Then she sniffed, and allowed herself the very faintest of smiles.

Unfortunately I don't have a magic wand, and there was no way I could remove Gilly's crushing pain that day. She was hurting terribly at her rejection – and at the thought of carving a life for herself without a husband. But what I did help her to see was that her irrational thoughts were making her feel even worse. And from that moment, she began to accept that recovery was possible and that she could learn the happiness habit.

Irrational thoughts are responsible for much of our unhappiness.

Section (f) Sex

This section is in the quiz so that you'll take a fresh look at what sex and intimacy are doing for you. Often people don't realise just how much their love lives have gone downhill till they're confronted by their answers.

Sometimes things have deteriorated so badly that where they once swigged champagne and swung naked from the chandelier, they now settle for cocoa, a quilted dressing gown and a swift 'goodnight' peck on the cheek!

Of course there's nothing wrong with having a quieter sex life if you're happy about it. And there's certainly nothing wrong with not having sex at all, if you're both agreed on that, or indeed if you're between relationships. No, the sadness comes when sex has become routine or boring, and you *do* care, but you don't know how to stem the decline.

It's also very distressing if you have to admit that sex has *never* really worked for you.

Of course you may be like Andrew, whose sex and relationship answers demonstrate that these are the happiest and healthiest areas in his whole life. But for many people, this section of the quiz will face them with unpalatable truths that – temporarily – cause them even more misery. I say temporarily, because admitting to a problem is always the first step in solving it. And because sex is so important, and so central to our emotional happiness, I'm devoting the whole of Chapter Eight to it.

But right now let's look at what your quiz answers mean.

If, for example, you answered 'often' to question 7, you can probably see for yourself that you're using sex in an unwise and unhealthy way. People who give their bodies in order to gain power or popularity are not just unhappy, but desperately lacking in self-esteem. Please take it from me that this kind of sex can only compound your unhappiness.

I have a client who always has sex with men who're already spoken for. As you can imagine, there's very little joy in love-making like that. And every time she takes a guy to bed, he gets up afterwards and goes back to his official partner, leaving my client feeling more wretched than ever.

If I'm describing what *you* do, please stop this destructive behaviour and try instead to use this book to raise your own sense of worth.

Other questions in this section – numbers 1, 2 and 3 for example – are about performance and inclination. I'm afraid that sex is often a major casualty when folk feel miserable. Some men lose their erections, which makes them even more depressed. Then they often push their partners away, causing more misery and loneliness to themselves and also to the men or women in their lives.

Women also frequently have problems with arousal when they're unhappy, but sometimes they are still able to draw some comfort from feeling loved and being cuddled. So whether you're a man or a woman, if you're in a reasonably good sexual relationship, do try to keep it ticking over by having some physical contact and loving, even if it doesn't extend to full sex. The warmth of undemanding intimacy can be hugely rewarding at a difficult time.

Before I leave this section on sex, I must just say that a significant number of miserable people have been raped, or have suffered childhood sexual abuse. If this applies to you, particularly if you've never had any help with it, please look at the directory at the back of the book where you'll find some useful addresses and advice on further reading. You might want to get on with that right away.

Section (g) Job

These days our jobs figure hugely in our lives. There are more dual-income families than ever before and, certainly in the UK, we've embraced a culture of long working hours. Various studies show that it's quite common for employees to work more than fifty hours a week – and then to take work home in the evenings and weekends too.

This is fine if you're feeling stimulated and happy. But very frequently such a workload leads to much stress and misery in other parts of your life.

So, looking at your quiz, the first point I must make is that if you have masses of 'often' answers in this section, maybe there's a case to be made for changing your job.

An impossible dream? Maybe. But try asking yourself these questions:

- Do you want to spend long hours all day – every day – doing something you hate?
- Do you think your job is secure for life?
- If it is, do you think that you'll ever feel more positive about it than you do today?
- And if it's not – and you're miserable in it – might it not be a good idea to move on sooner rather than later?

Of course, many people under forty do have to sacrifice their private lives temporarily to their career development – and you're not likely to be able to buck this trend, even if you agree it's an unhealthy one. But if you've put work first for years, yet somehow the career advancement you planned has failed to materialise, then I hope that your quiz answers will encourage you to take a fresh look at where you're going with your job – and your life.

Many people stick in a job believing that they cannot do without the accompanying status and salary. But all too often the pursuit of these things ruins relationships and other chances of happiness.

If you truly hate your work, try this little exercise: write down all the expenditure that you incur as a result of doing it. There are the lunches, the business clothes, the shoe repairs, the child care, the subscriptions to useful organisations or magazines, fares, income tax, pension funds etc. This kind of list can be a real eye-opener and can help you to comprehend fully – sometimes for the first time – just how much of your money is ploughed back into your job, and how little you get to keep and use.

There's a time in many women's working lives when compiling this list is especially useful, and that is when you've had a baby and find that the return to work is tearing at your emotions.

Many mums are convinced that they'll be longing to get back to their jobs soon after the birth. Some achieve this, and are excellent at organising their lives. They feel they have the best of both worlds, where they enjoy adult company and stimulus by day and family life at night and weekends.

But for every woman who's well adjusted to this lifestyle, there's another who feels tearful about being away from her child, and who starts to perceive her job in a much more negative way once she has an infant to focus on. I've known several successful women who wilted when they returned to work after their maternity leave. If this rings a bell with you, do compile the financial list. It can often give your struggle a whole new perspective.

The bottom line is that most of us need to work – so we force ourselves to stay in employment that we dislike, and to make the best of the situation. And this can often seem the most viable option, for a while. After all, even in the worst jobs there are compensations like the money and the friends you make among your colleagues. But the question is, have you sacrificed your family, or your personal happiness, for too long? If your quiz answers show that you're not really miserable in general, but that you *are* specifically fed up with your job, I hope you'll take this opportunity to rethink what you *really* want to do with the working part of your life.

Section (h) Your values

This section is in the quiz because I'm convinced that much of modern unhappiness is worsened by people dismissing qualities like charity, courtesy and decency as old-fashioned, and no longer worth bothering with.

Most of us have probably experienced a situation where our instinct has been to 'do the decent thing', but we've fought against it in case we're being wimpish.

We sometimes think that 'you've got to be a bit of a bastard to get on'. And that 'you've got to look after number one if you want to succeed'.

Actually, I believe very strongly that we *should* look after ourselves, but if we keep doing it at the expense of others, it ultimately makes us miserable. No one can feel true happiness if they go against what they intrinsically believe to be fair and honourable.

Of course many very decent people have totally different values from their mums and dads. This in itself is no bad thing. A recent study showed that young people today swear a great deal more than their parents or grandparents did, and that they see nothing wrong with that. It also showed that these same young people are much less racist and much more liberal than young people of twenty or so years ago. Personally I see these changes as very positive ones, though not everyone would agree.

So, do you know what *you* value? Or are you a bit at sea?

Unhappy people, for example, frequently answer 'often' to questions 3, 5 and 8. They tell me that they have no time, or money, or inclination to help others, or that they just can't be bothered because they can't see the point.

In their misery, their feelings are understandable, but unfortunately if we focus totally inwards, we become hideously self-pitying, and we also tend to reinforce our fears that we are bad and horrible – and that we don't deserve to be happy.

Yet the interesting thing is that most people who have these bitter feelings – and who have written themselves off as selfish and uncaring and inadequate – actually have very honourable beliefs deep down. Frequently too, they are generous to others. It's just they don't count these moments of goodness, because they are so disgusted with what they perceive as their own irredeemably bad behaviour.

When someone comes to me in this dejected state I always try to put him or her in touch with their own goodness. They may be convinced that they have no decency and that they are mean and unkind, but they almost always have hidden good traits that they're not aware of.

I had a client whom I'll call Carol. She had been a key figure in the Human Resources Department of a big company, but her firm was taken over and she was made redundant.

Carol was very depressed, and her misery was exacerbated by the fact that she mentally beat herself around the head over everything. It was *her* fault she had been made redundant. It was *her* fault that she had no man. *She* was a horrid and worthless person – and so it went on.

One day I asked her about 'good' things she had done. She looked at me as though I were mad. You could see her thinking that I must have been asleep while she had been cataloguing all the shortcomings in her terrible life!

She was very reluctant to dig deep into her soul to find anything positive, but I persisted.

Eventually she told me that when she had been working, she had always treated the junior members of her department to a really slap-up meal every year before Christmas.

'The company should have done something for them really,' she said. 'But they didn't. And I thought it was so awful that these women – who were not well paid – were not rewarded for the excellent work they did all the time, that I started my little tradition of the Christmas meal.'

'And did they like it?' I asked.

'Well, yes . . . they were quite overcome the first time . . . they clubbed together and bought me a beautiful vase the next day . . .'

There was a long pause here because Carol cried. She really cried – great gulping sobs. This was the first time she had wept in one of our sessions, despite all her sadness about losing her job. So what was it about this conversation that turned on the emotional taps?

She had found her vulnerable, soft side and it melted the harsh, self-critical and determinedly miserable veneer.

'So you're not really such a horrible, hopeless person at all,' I murmured.

Carol couldn't speak, but there was a different expression in her eyes – a mixture of hope and pain and possibilities.

'And perhaps you remembered their birthdays too?' I ventured.

She sniffed and grabbed a tissue and then she smiled, 'Well, I did, actually.'

Interestingly, that was the turning point in Carol's therapy. She began to accept that she was a kind person who was aware of the needs of others – and she then realised that a lot of the time she was punishing herself unnecessarily. As a result of her discovery, she really started to reach for happiness for herself.

So, if *you're* confused about your values, try to be aware of the good that you do. And if you honestly feel that you're too fed up and too mean to ever help anyone else – and that you feel bitter about your life – try to think of some contribution you can make to an individual in particular, or to society in general. Believe me, a sullen, totally self-interested person can never, ever be happy. But there is decency in us all: we just need to recognise and nurture it in order to be well-rounded individuals who are at peace in our own skins.

Section (i) Inner life
This section is a natural progression from the last one and it's all about how you choose to feed your soul. Many people nowadays have no time for organised religion. In that way, we may differ considerably from our parents and grandparents. But our inner life still needs to be nurtured.

We can find beauty and emotional succour from all sorts of items and happenings: for example, the first flower of spring in the garden. But often when people feel very sad, they resist the call of their souls. Naturally if they refuse to be moved by anything, they miss out on a lot and become even sadder.

There have always been sad people, but until recently far fewer folk had any real expectations of happiness. Up till about eighty years ago, average, fairly impoverished working people rarely questioned whether or not they were happy. Life was generally considered to be what you put up with while you waited for the joys of heaven!

Nowadays of course we don't believe we should tolerate abject misery, poverty, abuse and a lack of fulfilment in the hope that we might be rewarded when we die. We want to make all these things better *now*.

It's certainly no bad thing to want happiness in this life – I wouldn't be writing this book if I thought it were. But I don't think that true contentment is possible today unless we work at developing our whole selves – mind, body and spirit.

Earlier in this chapter, I asked you to set aside ten minutes every day for peaceful thinking and relaxation. But once this has become a habit, I'd like to encourage you to go beyond that and find yourself even more personal time and space, because I'm utterly convinced that no one can achieve real abiding happiness until they can value quiet times entirely alone.

Frequently, miserable and stressed-out people come for therapy who can hardly even find time for their appointments with me because of their busy schedules. They have hectic jobs and equally hectic social lives. In fact I remember one client who thought she was a complete failure if she ever found herself alone. And if the weekend was looming and she had no party plans in place, she got into a terrible panic. The truth was she was terrified of solitude.

But by chasing happiness so hard, she was ignoring her inner self. So I suggested she spend some time alone. She looked stricken; but eventually she agreed not to make arrangements to meet friends during the daylight hours of the following Saturday, but to potter round an antique market instead.

When I saw her the following week, she looked genuinely more peaceful and pleased with life, and she reported that she'd actually enjoyed the experiment. As a consequence, she began spending more time alone – going to the cinema and art galleries and meandering round the park in her lunch hour.

She didn't stop being gregarious, but she *did* stop having to be gregarious all the time. And once she could just 'be' on her own, she found a contentment that had previously eluded her.

So, what can you do to feed your inner being? Well, obviously if you take part in any organised religion, there are plenty of places where you can find some solace. Personally I love to go to a large church or cathedral and find a quiet, dark corner and listen to the choir singing. For me this is immensely refreshing and sustaining.

Other people find similar peace through meditation, or through religions other than Christianity. Still more are nurtured by music, painting, the sea, the countryside and so on. And, from experience, I can vouch for the fact that hypnosis and self-hypnosis provide a wonderful sense of relaxation.

In a sense it doesn't matter what you choose. What does matter is that you acknowledge the demands of your soul and act upon them.

Section (j) Family

This section of the quiz asks questions that are almost bound to cause you pain. Our families, which should be our surest base of love and support, are so often the source of contention and misery.

I would go so far as to say that whenever I see a client who is distressed, one of the parents of that client is always a palpable presence in the consulting room. With men it's usually the father who is there, and with women, it's generally the mother – but not invariably. These mums or dads seem to perch on the shoulders of my poor clients, weighing them down. Sometimes I wish they were actually there: I'd like to strangle a few of them!

I'm not trying to get all Freudian here, but the fact is that it's rare to be able to treat a patient's unhappiness without delving into the kind of parenting they had, and without exploring the client's feelings about one or other parent.

I feel that the most emotional questions in the whole quiz are in this family section; and they are the ones which ask whether or not your father or mother loved you enough. Many people who are unhappy feel very short-changed in these parental-loving stakes, and answering the questions often brings out tears and sadness.

If you have problems in this area, let me assure you that you are far from being alone, and also that you can overcome your difficulties. We have to learn to accept our parents for what they are, or were – and that means it's OK to acknowledge that perhaps parenting was not their strong point.

Sometimes when you do that, a great weight rolls off you.

We all have such emotional baggage about our good, indifferent and frankly lousy parenting that I'll be devoting a whole chapter to the subject later in the book.

But to return to the quiz – I also asked questions about you as a parent. When people are miserable – and especially if their relationships are in trouble – it's not uncommon for them to occasionally wish that they'd never had children.

This secret admission usually gives rise to terrible guilt. But if answering the quiz has uncovered these kinds of emotions, please don't despair. By dedicating yourself to finding and developing your happiness habit, you will soon feel more complete and rounded as a person, and this will help you to resolve difficulties in your relationships, and with your kids.

Section (k) Interests

The 'interests' section is all about how much joy you're able to find currently in activities you normally enjoy. So, how did you fare?

If you answered 'often' to question 3, you need to start balancing your life by mixing with people more. Happiness is all about balance. And though I've encouraged you in this chapter to find lots of peaceful time and space for yourself, too much of it will turn you into a loner. So if you're avoiding people, try to make some effort to spend time in the company of others.

If you've answered 'often' to the other questions, I'm afraid this shows that you are very low, and that you're finding it difficult to summon the effort to enjoy your leisure time.

Sadly, this is a common state of affairs when people are fed up. Miserable people frequently complain that they can't concentrate, or that they have no appetite for their usual hobbies. They also tend to answer 'often' to question 5 about stopping themselves from feeling enjoyment. They say that there's no point allowing themselves to feel pleasure, because that pleasure doesn't represent how they really feel. They perceive it as a sham.

I hope you can see that this is *very* depressed thinking. It's also very negative, and can only make misery worse.

As I keep saying, it's important, even when you're unhappy, to find some enjoyment in your life. Life may be absolutely bloody, but you can still have moments of pleasure in it. Wouldn't you sooner have some than none?

Earlier in this chapter I asked you to look out for five happy moments every day. Now I want you to go one step further by 'doing' an activity twice a week that you really enjoy. This should be something which is guaranteed to lift your mood even at the worst of times. It can be hard to get started, but persevere and I guarantee you'll start to feel better.

You can select a pastime as undemanding as listening to music that gets your feet tapping. You can choose tapestry – so long as you really enjoy such an intricate hobby. You can take up the piano, even if you're not very good at it. Or you might decide to re-make your window box into a riot of colour and splendour. Whatever you choose, do it because you like it, and then allow the slivers of joy it brings you to feed your happiness habit.

Section (l) Friends

I deliberately included a section on friends in the quiz because when we're miserable we often shut ourselves away and neglect our friends. Then we feel aggrieved because they neglect us in return!

There are two questions in this section which are just as much about self-esteem as about friendship. So if you've answered 'often' to questions 7 and 8, do focus on Chapter Six when you get to it, because it will certainly help you.

Friendship is so vital to our happiness. But we sometimes forget – especially when we're very down – that to have a friend, you have to be a friend. We want help from our friends, but we just don't realise that friendship cannot survive as one-way traffic. So even when life is going badly, it's always worth making an effort to be with friends, and to make those friendships as 'equal' as possible.

Let me tell you about Suzy. She complained to me that she was not only very miserable, but that her best friend was getting fed up with her.

At first hearing the friend sounded incredibly callous. After all, these two women had known each other since their university days, some six years previously.

But when we talked about it, I realised that Suzy had given up being an active friend, and that she had come to expect her pal, Elizabeth, to make the friendship work.

It turned out that Elizabeth had a happy marriage and a career as a television researcher. But she was very, very busy. And she didn't earn much.

My client, Suzy, had inherited some money – not a fortune, but enough to keep her solvent – but she had no partner, and just worked part-time.

In her misery, she envied Elizabeth. She saw her friend as much more capable, much happier and much luckier. So she sat back and expected Elizabeth to make all the arrangements for their meetings and to pay for them too. Not surprisingly, Elizabeth began to feel used.

At first sight then, this friendship didn't seem to have much going for it. But I knew that Suzy was desperate to retain it, and I suspected that deep down, Elizabeth probably wanted to preserve it too.

I suggested to Suzy that her friend was probably feeling a bit hard done by. I also pointed out just how little a television researcher earns. I also tried to impress on Suzy that if she continued to shirk responsibility for this important friendship, she would lose it.

She was aghast at the way I interpreted the situation, but soon she began to realise how her very 'down' feelings had led her to lean unfairly on her friend. It simply hadn't occurred to her that she needed to put effort into their friendship, or that Elizabeth might need support and love and care from her – let alone a bit of financial consideration occasionally.

Luckily it wasn't too late to rescue the relationship and we agreed that the two women would, from now on, meet at Suzy's flat –

which was comfortable and central – and that Suzy would provide a meal and bottle of wine!

What Elizabeth would provide was her cheering presence, her energy, her tales from work and her time – which was in extremely short supply.

Once these two women – who genuinely loved each other – could see how they could both feed the friendship and therefore both sustain it, their relationship entered a new phase and they are now better mates than ever.

But isn't it alarming to contemplate how very nearly this long-term friendship fizzled out – mainly because Suzy had got to the point where she undervalued herself so badly that she had stopped contributing to it. And of course, losing Elizabeth as a pal would have compounded her misery.

Happiness takes effort – I'm sure you know that by now. And friendship takes a lot of effort too. Fortunately, Suzy grasped these concepts and she gradually turned into a much more self-reliant and buoyant person as a result.

Of course, there are times when you are extremely low when it's perfectly OK – even desirable – to garner all the support you can get from friends, without worrying about giving much back.

But the rest of the time we must give as much to our friends as we hope to receive. And we must make the effort to cherish them, even when we're happy and busy – because we'll certainly need them when we're not.

Section (m) The future

The questions in this section about the future are very difficult to cope with for miserable people. But I do hope that you haven't answered 'often' to question 8 about waiting for happiness to happen. The whole thrust of this book is about helping yourself to happiness – not expecting it to flow down on you from the skies. Stop waiting – you'll wait a long time!

If you've answered 'often' to questions 1 and 2, I'm afraid you are very low – but then you probably know that. But as you get to work with the tasks in this book, you will alter your perception of the future and it will start to look rosier.

Believe me, I do know that it takes a huge shift of mood to accept that today's lousy feelings and set of circumstances can one day be better. It needs an act of faith – and that in itself requires mental energy that sad people don't always feel they have.

I deliberately put a question about Christmas into this section because it is such a terrible time for unhappy people. In fact when I was at my worst, I used to start dreading Christmas around February! New Year was nearly as bad.

Any agony aunt will tell you that Christmas and New Year get people in a right tizz. It's not just that you're supposed to have a great time, and that you tend to believe the whole world is merrily celebrating while you feel you're drowning in misery. It's also that these are landmark times. So we tend to say, 'God, I can't believe I'm still in this hateful job – and it's nearly Christmas'; or, 'It's New Year – and I can't bear the fact that I'm still in this affair . . .'

So the 'festive' season is difficult – and so are thoughts of the future. But please take hold of the fact that even the very saddest among us can achieve happiness again. I've lost count of the number of rejected people I've known, written to, treated and met on television programmes, who felt that their lives were at an end, and who later worked at their happiness till they became much more contented and interesting than they'd ever been before.

I've seen this so often that I know there's no reason why it shouldn't happen for you. Your life has not been pre-ordained in its awfulness. You can change it, and I hope you're beginning to understand that.

Now I want you to tackle one more task, which will help your happiness habit no end.

Earlier in this chapter I encouraged you to look out for, and to enjoy, five happy moments every day. I also asked you to help your quest for happiness by tackling an enjoyable hobby at least twice a week.

If you do these tasks regularly – and I hope you've already begun – you'll soon have far more happy moments in your life than you had before. In fact you'll have thirty-five moments and at least two pleasurable activities under your belt every week!

So what I want you to do now is to review every single one of these happy happenings once a week – maybe on a Saturday – and to select the week's highlights. Think what touched you most. Was it the fair-haired chubby toddler who was laughing uncontrollably as he jumped in and out of puddles? Or was it the moment when you ran a whole mile for the first time? Go through each day remembering the good bits, and when you've recalled everything, pick the very best three or four memories. These are your treasures of the week – and I want you to cherish them.

This is what you do next: imagine a large, jewel-encrusted and velvet-lined casket. This is the new home for your 'treasures'. So every week when you select your best moments, you can tuck them away in this imaginary box.

Now that these happy moments have a special place of their own you can really value them. In fact they can bring you joy at any time, because you can withdraw them and look at them and re-live them at will – even on the roughest of days.

One of the treasures in my casket, for example, is a sunny afternoon in my garden. It's all a bit overgrown and untidy – because I'm no gardener – but it's a soothing, lovely, familiar place and in the summer, my husband and I enjoy having meals out there – especially tea in the afternoons. So that's a very evocative treasure for me and one I can draw out from its imaginary safe place on a dark, wintry day when my mood isn't as upbeat as it should be!

Your casket is the final task of this chapter. I've asked you to do a lot in these last few pages. And I've asked you to grasp rather a lot too. But all this hard work will be worth it – I promise!

Chapter Two Key Points:

- Concentrate on the happiness you have in life instead of dwelling on your unhappiness.
- Find five happy moments every day.
- Spend ten minutes daily on The Ten-Minute Soother – just sitting and thinking pleasant thoughts.
- If you're lacking in self-esteem, greet three new strangers daily.
- Try to build some exercise into your routine and eat five pieces of fruit per day.
- Indulge yourself by doing two activities a week that you enjoy.
- Take more responsibility for your moods – and for finding happiness, even on difficult days.
- Learn to stop worrying about things and events which you have no power to alter.
- Build your happiness week by week – using your imaginary casket to treasure your good moments.

3

Happiness Comes from Putting Right What You Can, and Accepting What You Can't

It's difficult to recognise aspects of your life that you can change and to learn to accept those that you can't — but once you train yourself to divide your problems into these two groups, your happiness rating will immediately improve.

Many human problems are actually a *combination* of changeable and unchangeable components. Here's a simple example.

Neil is five foot two inches tall and he weighs eighteen stone. He *hates* how he looks.

Neil's problem is two-pronged: he is shorter than he'd like to be, but he can do nothing about that. He is also fatter than he'd like to be, and that is a situation he *does* have the power to alter. So he needs to accept one circumstance and vow to change the other.

Life's difficulties rarely, alas, present themselves in such easily defined categories, but with practice we can learn to look at them objectively, and to work out where there's scope for change and where there isn't.

If we don't make this distinction, we usually end up feeling pretty downcast about all sorts of things.

And what's worse is that when we refuse to take responsibility for our troubles in life, we frequently resort to completely illogical statements that are no help to ourselves, or anyone else.

These include:

- It's not fair!
- Everything happens to me!
- Life's a bitch!
- No one understands me.
- No one appreciates me.
- It's all right for some.

I remember a passage in a book I read as a teenager – unfortunately I've long since forgotten which book it was – where a young mum said that the best way to prepare a child for life was to put him on a high sideboard, invite him to jump into your arms and then walk away so that he crashed to the floor. She said that there was no better method for demonstrating to an infant that life *isn't* fair.

I'm not endorsing this method! But we'd all be a lot happier if we accepted that life is *not* fair. No one ever promised that it would be.

Of course some people are born brainier than others are. Some are more naturally beautiful. Others have untold inherited wealth. But we cannot alter these facts, and if we dwell on them and allow ourselves to feel that 'life is unfair', all we do is hurt ourselves.

So, 'It's not fair!' has got to go. Similarly, get rid of all those phrases that make you sound whiny and sorry for yourself. If, for example, you're having a bad day at the office and you explode with a cry of: 'Everything happens to me' or, worse still: 'No one around here appreciates me', your colleagues will probably raise their eyes heavenward and mutter: 'Here she goes again.' You won't get any sympathy and you'll probably be perceived as someone who's negative and chaotic – and a right moaner to boot. So lose these phrases!

It's also vital to cut out all those sayings that indicate you're eaten up with envy – which is a pointless emotion. Frequently people with mean, down-turned mouths mutter: 'It's all right for some', when they're not only feeling that life is unfair but when they're jealous of someone else's good fortune. Such an expression has no power to damage the folk we're jealous of, but it very definitely damages – and sometimes even destroys – us.

So, if you want to be positive and happy, do yourself a great favour and banish negative phrases from your lips, and pointless and destructive emotions – like envy and bitterness – from your heart. You *can* do this, and you'll be much, much happier as a result.

Horrible Humphrey hasn't learned any of these things.

He's an actor: not a bad one as it happens, but he has a terrible attitude. He's married to a young friend of mine called Lisa.

For several years I've listened to Lisa extolling her husband's talents and bemoaning the fact that no one recognises how brilliant he really is. Humphrey doesn't work a lot – nothing so unusual in that, since plenty of extremely talented actors are unemployed much of the time. But Humphrey has the added disadvantage that he's excessively difficult.

Lisa has always been very loyal when she's spoken of him, but even so, details of Humphrey's dysfunctional behaviour have gradually emerged over the years. He's childishly petulant. He can't stand noise and makes a ridiculous fuss when neighbours are putting up shelves, or the dustmen are collecting the bins. He never helps with shopping or housework even though he's 'resting' at home a lot. He lets Lisa pay for everything. Worst of all, he never tries to see the best in people, and he certainly never attempts to make positive changes, or to accept that there are inequalities in life that we cannot alter.

Poor Lisa. Whenever Humphrey lands a small part in a television drama, or in the theatre, she prays that *this* time he'll get on well with everyone, and, more importantly, that this job will lead to better work.

There's usually a honeymoon period of about three days at the new job during which Humphrey is charm itself. But then his moaning starts and it generally focuses on the star of the show. Filled with negative envy of the lead actor, Humphrey will criticise him for drinking too much, or for being temperamental, or for being too friendly, or for seeming aloof while he learns his lines. He'll also complain about how much this celebrity is being paid and will invariably rubbish the other actor's talent. In fact it wouldn't really matter what the guy did because Humphrey would find fault with him somehow.

Lisa has heard all this so often, but until recently she always kept it to herself. But last month she reached breaking point and came to see me in tears.

'I've just realised something, Christine,' she whimpered. 'All these years I thought that "everything happened to Humphrey" – because that's how *he* sees it. I also thought, as he does, that life's particularly unfair to him. But suddenly it's hit me that all these things can't always be everyone else's fault. He just doesn't take responsibility for anything. He always sees the worst in everyone and never for one moment thinks that he's to blame, or that he could take a different attitude and get on much better – and be happier.'

No one could have been more supportive than Lisa, but she's had enough – and I don't blame her. She's decided to divorce him.

Will Horrible Humphrey come to his senses and realise that he himself is making his life unfair, and that he himself could change it? I hope so, but I'm not holding my breath.

Lisa, on the other hand, has learned an important lesson. She has finally realised that she can change things about herself – like she can leave her horrid husband – but that she *cannot* change Humphrey.

Women like to change men – no doubt about it. It's one of our favourite hobbies! In fact it's common for a really lovely woman to attach herself to distinctly unpromising male material, believing that with her power and persuasion, she'll turn him into the ideal husband! When the guy stubbornly refuses to change, and Lovely-Woman realises she's hitched to a flawed human rather than Super-

Sensitive-New-Man, the relationship often goes sour.

I've lost count of the number of females I know who have told me things like: 'Once we're married, I won't let him go to all those football matches'; or: 'When we're living together I'll put a stop to all those nights in the pub he has with his mates.' Then they're amazed when their partners continue to do exactly what they've always done.

A male psychologist friend of mine sums up the difference in the genders with this story. A man takes a woman back to his place for the first time. His body is ready for sex and his mind is focused on getting it. For the time being, the woman in his arms seems like a perfect goddess. Meanwhile, this perfect goddess is lying beside him thinking: 'What hideous curtains. They'll have to go!'

I have to admit that there's more than a grain of truth in this story.

Certainly in my psychotherapeutic practice, women often come asking how to change their partners' behaviour. They'll say: 'I'm unhappy because my husband shows me no affection, so I want you to tell me how to change him.'

Therapy doesn't work like that and I have to explain to my new client that the only person who's guaranteed to change during the course of counselling is her.

Of course, sometimes when a woman does a lot of work on herself, her partner does change. For instance, as she becomes more confident, more assertive and more attractive, he may well respond to the 'new' her by being more attentive. Usually this change arises out of fear as he begins to twig that his partner has stopped being a doormat and that he might just lose her!

But no one can bank on anyone else changing. Often they don't. In therapy, as in life, we must learn to put right what we *can* and accept what we *can't*.

Caroline used to be a miserable person. She never took responsibility for the things she could change, but she used to expect changes to happen miraculously in events or circumstances that were never going to alter – or that were beyond her control. It took a day of disasters for her to see the light!

On that day, unusually for her, she drove to work instead of taking the train.

She didn't allow sufficient time for her journey and was running very late by the time she drew up at her office. So, instead of putting her motor into a long-term car park some distance away, she left it in a meter space much nearer her building – even though this meant she'd have to move it at lunchtime.

She spent most of the morning feeling rushed and upset because of her late arrival. She also kept telling herself how unfair life was. After all, she was doing her best, wasn't she? But she felt jangled and hurried and clumsy. First of all she knocked her coffee all over some important papers, then she loaded the photocopier too swiftly and jammed it. *Everything* happened to her!

At lunchtime she went to a local café. She tried to enjoy her sandwich and to relax by reading the paper, but the minutes ticked by and she couldn't stop worrying about moving the car.

When she came to pay, there was a long queue at the till and she grew more and more impatient as she waved her £20 note in the direction of the cashier. Eventually it was her turn. Thrusting her change – without looking at it – into her jacket pocket, she ran outside and along the pavement to her car. Thankfully there was one minute left on the meter. But just as she unlocked the door, she realised that the cashier in the café had only given her change for £10 instead of £20.

Cursing, she crashed the gears and reversed jerkily out of her space – right into the path of an oncoming motor. Her heart sank as she heard a loud blast on a horn and the inevitable crunch.

Trembling and tearful she swapped insurance details with the other driver, who, not surprisingly, was extremely annoyed at the damage Caroline had inflicted on his vehicle.

By the time she had pacified him and driven to the long-term car park, she was half an hour late back at the office. Her boss murmured something about her 'unprofessional attitude' as he grudgingly accepted her apology.

In the quiet of the Ladies' Room, Caroline cried.

At first she went into her usual 'it's not fair' mode of thinking. It wasn't fair that there'd been so much traffic this morning. It wasn't fair that her boss was so cranky. It wasn't fair that the café had been so crowded. It wasn't fair that she'd been short-changed to the tune of £10, and it certainly wasn't fair that just when she was backing her car out of the meter slot, another vehicle had materialised out of nowhere.

Suddenly she caught sight of herself in the mirror above the wash basin. She could see a face – streaked with tears – that had bitterness etched into every pore. And in a flash she resolved to stop being the negative person who was staring back out of her.

I was late this morning, she thought, and that was down to me – nobody else: I should have left much earlier. It was my decision to park where I did, and though it wasn't totally my fault that I was short-changed, it was my fault that I wasn't concentrating. If I had been, I could have pointed out the error there and then, whereas now it's too late. It was entirely up to me that I was rushing to re-park like a mad thing and without a doubt I, and no one else, caused the prang.

I could have changed most of these things, she thought, but I didn't. Now I can't change them. I wish they hadn't happened, but I have to accept that they did.

Caroline took a deep breath and waited for more tears to fall. And then, as she told me later, a really surprising emotion swept over her. Instead of feeling more sad and hopeless at the thought that she had engineered her own disasters, she suddenly felt as though a weight had rolled off her shoulders.

This is my life, she thought to herself. It's up to me what happens in it and it's time I took charge of it. And from that moment, Caroline began to feel happier and to realise that it was within her power to make important changes.

The very next morning, she noticed an advert for a marketing job in the paper. Prior to that day she might have considered trying for it, but she would have told herself that, with her luck, she'd never get it.

But with her new zeal for taking responsibility for her life and happiness, she applied for it. And when she was granted an interview, she not only prepared for it thoroughly, but she talked herself into believing that she had the ability to land it.

After all, she reasoned, someone has to get it. Why not me? More than that, she began to see that she was not helping anyone, least of all herself, by being negative. She came to the conclusion that not only would it be perfectly appropriate for her to get the job – because she would do it well – but that she would be able to contribute more to her life, and to the life of others, once she had more power and money.

She suddenly saw with absolute clarity that for years she had been waiting for happiness, but not doing anything to alter her circumstances. She could also see that she had never put her energy into change, and also that she had allowed herself to go through life expecting the worst, and then dwelling on her bad luck when the worst happened.

Having prepared thoroughly for the interview, Caroline turned up for it in plenty of time, looking attractive and well-groomed. She then relaxed, confident that she had done all she could, and accepting that the outcome was now in somebody else's hands. She got the job!

Caroline has continued to feel happier for months now, and all because she has come to understand that there are always things we can change, but some that we can't.

I'd like to take the credit for Caroline's transformation, because we'd often talked together about positive thinking. But when it came to it, she grasped the concept of responsibility and happiness on her own. She did it her way – and she's a much more rounded individual as a result. Now she sees for herself that there are always things that we can change, and some that we cannot.

However, for some people, accepting the pack of cards that life has dealt them is a very tough challenge, particularly when the attitude of people around them is unhelpful.

Twenty-eight-year-old Alana is just such a person. She has asthma. This is controllable, but not curable. She also has diabetes. Again this is manageable, but she has to inject with insulin every day, which means that she can never forget her condition. It's been hard for her to come to terms with her ill health, which, to some extent, prevents her from leading a totally normal life.

Alana doesn't want to feel that she has no potential, but it's been difficult for her to break out of the lack of expectation that surrounds her. For example, her parents, who have always found her disabilities hard to accept, have never discussed the possibility of Alana getting married or having children, while they talk of such things with her younger sister all the time.

Another problem has been that Alana never felt she could have a career – because her family never seemed to have any ambition for her. As a result, after leaving school Alana had a succession of office jobs in which she had absolutely no interest.

One week short of her twenty-ninth birthday, her firm 'rational-ised' its staff numbers and she was one of those who lost their jobs.

For a couple of days she cried and she swore and thought how unfair her life was. And let's face it, who wouldn't have felt the same in her situation? Fortunately, Alana is very resilient, in her quiet way. She began to see that because of her parents' limited view of what was available to a 'disabled' person, she had taken one job after another that she hated. Suddenly it occurred to her that while there were aspects to her life that could never be changed – like her illnesses – there were others that could be. She could grow into the person she wanted to be and she could get a job that she liked.

Three years later she is transformed. She had always loved children, but had previously believed that her poor health would prevent her from working with them. But she's now helping at a school for blind kids and is soon off to do a full-time course to become a teacher.

In a quite stunning way, Alana has grasped chances for change wherever she could, and she has fully accepted those areas of her life that are not going to alter, like her medical condition. She is a happy person now. She no longer thinks of herself as a victim. And despite the fact that she does not enjoy good health, she's stopped feeling that life is unfair.

Most of all, she has refused to accept boundaries set by other people who couldn't cope with the woman she wanted to become, and she feels affirmed by doing work that she's good at, with people who really need her.

People with obvious illnesses or disabilities have more work to do on accepting unchangeable facets of their lives than the rest of us. So it's remarkable how often someone with physical difficulties is astonishingly cheerful and positive – and not at all self-pitying.

But what about all those regrettable parts of our lives that we cannot change – but that we know, deep down, we've inflicted on ourselves?

I'm thinking in particular of those uncomfortable memories we're left with when we've said or done something we regret and we can't put it right. Frequently we try to justify our words or our actions to ourselves, or we attempt to forget the incident, but somehow, it just keeps niggling away, and making us feel guilty, and spoiling our happiness.

Many people, for example, carry a weighty burden of guilt at having been impatient with a dying or demented parent at the end of his or her life. Or at having wished a sick parent, or even a partner, dead.

'If only I'd been kinder,' they cry.

Others have deep misgivings about how they got out of their marriages. They feel that in their emotional turmoil they were often unjustifiably unkind to their partners.

'I just couldn't handle my feelings,' one man told me. 'So I hit out at my wife because – as I saw it at the time – she was standing in the way of my happiness.'

Personally, I think that in order to move on and find contentment, it's vital to accept that we were responsible for these actions – and, wherever possible, to discuss them in confidence with someone else. Furthermore, I firmly believe that it's an excellent idea to 'pay' for our misdeeds in some way. This kind of gesture aids our mental health and happiness.

It's no accident that in many of the world's religions there is an accepted procedure for facing our faults and wrongdoings, confessing them, asking forgiveness and then accepting some penitential task or other as a means of atoning for them. But I'm convinced that even people who have no obvious allegiance to any religion can find peace within themselves if they atone for their 'wrongdoing', or try to put it right, in some appropriate way.

Some methods of atonement are clear-cut – though they might seem unpalatable. Obviously, for example, if you were an embezzler and you were troubled by what you'd done, you could repay the money!

Family arguments, on the other hand, are harder to sort out. Yet they're very common and are often a source of pain and anxiety.

If you've had a serious quarrel with a member of your own family – perhaps you haven't spoken to them for years – you'll know how hurtful this estrangement can be, and how it tends to bother you at special times like Christmas and birthdays and New Year.

Wouldn't it be good to make the first move towards a reconciliation – even if you still feel that the original fight was not your fault? Wouldn't it salve your conscience? And wouldn't you feel more at peace with yourself, even if the worst happened and the other party couldn't forgive and forget? I think you would. You might consider trying it.

Naturally, if you've wronged someone who's died, a rapprochement is impossible. And the feeling of hopelessness that you're too late to change something for the better can be agonising.

But you can acknowledge that you feel genuine remorse. Also, if you want to, you can share that feeling with someone you trust. Finally, you can decide on some suitable gesture to express your sorrow at what happened.

You could put flowers on the dead person's grave, for example. Or you could give some care and time to someone that the dead person loved, or you could make a donation to a charity that the dead person used to support.

These actions won't alter the original wrong, but they will help you to put it behind you and to get on with your life.

We all make mistakes – that's another aspect of ourselves that we have to accept. But to let these errors ruin our lives is the worst mistake of all. So, alter what you can, and make reparation the best way possible, then seek forgiveness – and, above all, forgive yourself.

But what if you've wronged someone who doesn't know what you've done? In this instance you might choose to confess your wrongdoing to them, to appease your guilt. But tread carefully, or you could end up doing more harm than good.

For example, if you'd had an affair with a married man, it might help *you* to tell his wife everything, and ask her forgiveness. But if she were blissfully unaware of her husband's infidelity, your confession would probably bring her untold grief.

A friend of mine was once badly hurt when a colleague bared her soul to her. My pal, Annie, was in her mid-thirties at the time and was a well-known television reporter. Unfortunately she was going through a period where she was very stressed and depressed, and, by her own admission, she was far too emotionally involved with a story she was working on about a missing child.

Eventually the child was found – dead. Annie was distraught. Her feelings were all mixed up with her own wish for children and her inability to find the right man to have them with. She was almost hysterical about the dead infant.

As she was sitting at her desk, trying to make some sense of the tragedy, a woman who worked in her newsroom confronted her.

'I just thought I'd tell you', she began, 'that I've been seeing a counsellor . . .'

Annie looked at her blankly, wondering what to say.

'Yes,' the woman went on. 'And I've been discussing with her how much I've always really hated you.'

'What?' Annie was completely bewildered.

'Yes. Always hated you with your wonderful job and your brains and nice looks and everything. So I decided to tell you how much I always hated you and how jealous I've always been of you – and do you know what?'

Annie shook her head.

'I feel better.'

Well, that newsroom employee *may* have felt better. But for my poor friend in her already fragile state the hatred of this female she hardly knew was like a dagger in her heart. And I was not the only one of Annie's friends who feared for her sanity, and indeed her life, for the next week or two.

So if you have some confessing to do, select your confessor carefully. A professional of some kind is generally a safer bet.

There are various life events which cause people particular guilt and grief. One of them is abortion.

I have to admit that as an agony aunt and psychotherapist I don't tend to hear from people if they're totally unfazed by having a termination. But time and time again, I do see and hear from women, and men, who feel terribly troubled because they've chosen to end a pregnancy.

In fact, when a woman comes into therapy complaining that she spends her whole time struggling with miserable feelings, there's often a termination in her history.

Sometimes clients will admit that they regret ending the pregnancy. But often they remain convinced that termination was the right choice, yet they are still left with a legacy of sadness and guilt and loss.

This definitely needs talking out, either in therapy, or with a priest or other religious advisor, or with a doctor, or even with a trusted close friend.

Many men and women are astonished at how much the termination has affected them. They had thought they were fully in charge of their lives and their destinies and their bodies, and their post-abortion misery makes them question whether they're actually in command of any of it.

When confronted by this kind of suffering, my belief is that we should accept that there are things connected with life and death that we cannot always explain or deal with by using our customary coping mechanisms.

And I believe that resorting to some kind of spiritual or ritualistic process can be valuable.

So, for example, when I am dealing with a client who has had a termination, I usually encourage her to mark various anniversaries of their aborted infant by lighting a candle in a church, or at home. And I also encourage her to appease her sense of guilt by sponsoring a foreign child, or by befriending a disadvantaged child in this country, or even by taking a special interest in a nephew or niece.

Termination, death and sometimes even divorce are events that can disturb our normal equilibrium for a long time. And even when they were absolutely necessary, they can still leave us with immense regret. So we have to acknowledge our feelings about them, before putting right what we can and accepting what we can't. But then we must move on.

No good purpose is served when we remain perpetual martyrs to our guilt, and allow unwise or wrong actions to ruin the rest of our lives.

It's often difficult – even terrifying – to face up to things that we bitterly regret having done. But the alternative is usually far worse. Remember: sorting some wrong you've done is a way of changing things for the better.

So change what you can, and accept what you can't – and happiness will follow.

Chapter Three Key Points:

- Wherever possible, change any problems or unhappiness in your life.
- Accept what you cannot change.
- When you have events in your past that you regret – like family quarrels – do your best to apologise and put them right.
- When there are events in your past that cannot be altered, face up to them, and talk about them; then try to atone for them in some way by doing something worthwhile and kind. Finally – let the past go.

4

Happiness Comes from Challenging Irrational Thinking

I bet when you were a kid, you used to torment yourself with irrational thoughts like: If I tread on the cracks in the pavement, I'll die. Or: If two more buses pass before I get to school, dad won't buy me that bike I want.

Such musings are OK when we're young, but we'd feel pretty silly thinking them as adults. And yet we do allow ourselves to entertain equally barmy thoughts every day of our lives – and these thoughts frequently inhibit our quest for happiness.

So, this chapter is all about challenging how we think, and asking ourselves where the evidence is for the way we're thinking.

The fact is that mostly we go through life believing that our thoughts arise as a result of the emotions we're feeling. Whereas the truth is that our thoughts *create* our emotions.

This is why I keep encouraging you to choose the happiness option whenever it's possible to do so, and also to re-train your thoughts so that you recognise happy moments when you have them.

I hope this re-training is working for you, and that already you're a happier person than you were when you bought the book. But to increase your happiness still further, I now want you to accept the main message of this chapter, which is that your thoughts – which are frequently illogical – are largely responsible for your unhappy feelings.

Albert Ellis, who's a very brilliant man and a pioneer of modern psychotherapeutic thinking, says: 'It's not THINGS that upset us. It's our VIEW of things.'

Another equally perceptive gentleman was thinking along the same lines very much earlier on. Epictetus was a Greek philosopher in the first century. His own life was far from idyllic as he was lame and also for a time was a slave in Rome. But in the midst of all this adversity he declared that happiness depends upon our ability to control such things as are in our power. He also believed that the views we take of things are much more upsetting than the things themselves.

To illustrate what Epictetus and Ellis were getting at, let's look at the example of three guys who all win the lottery one Saturday night.

All three of them are working men in their thirties or forties. None of them is wealthy. And each of them wins around three million pounds, so you might expect all their reactions to be similar. But they're not.

Man A is initially thrilled, but then he starts worrying that he will be pestered throughout his remaining life by charities and hangers on. As each hour goes by he becomes more and more anxious. Then he sees on the teletext that there are two other jackpot winners. He feels cruelly disappointed. I wish I'd won it all, he thinks. Then I'd have so much money I wouldn't have to worry about everyone asking for some.

Man B is shocked at the idea of being so rich. It should be great, but how will he know who his friends are? He hasn't got a wife, and how on earth will he choose one now, because he'll never know if someone wants him for himself, or for his money?

Man C is uncomplicatedly delighted. He's worked hard all his life and this win will mean he never has to worry about security again. On the back of an envelope he does a few sums calculating what it will cost to pay off his own mortgage and that of his two sons and daughter. He then lists some of his lifetime ambitions – all of which he can now afford – and decides that he'll fulfil them all, starting by taking his extended family off to the Caribbean for Christmas. He thinks he'll probably also buy a new car and that he might throw a party – and put the rest of the money into investments.

At that moment he notices that it's news time on the television. He watches a heart-rending report about a refugee crisis in middle Europe. He's very moved by the plight of these people, especially in the light of his own sudden good fortune. There and then he decides to donate £100,000 to the appeal. He feels hugely happy that he can afford to be this generous and is also pleased that from now on he'll be able to help people financially whenever he wants to.

So there you are: three men – and three completely different ways of responding to the same situation. And all because their separate views of the same thing have sparked off entirely different emotions. One of them has seized happiness; the other two are allowing all sorts of conflicting thoughts to ruin what should be a fantastic experience.

You might remember Gilly, the florist, whom I mentioned in Chapter Two. After her husband rejected her, her view of life was very warped, and her thinking was quite illogical.

Naturally she was miserable. Who wouldn't have been? But she made herself unhappier than she need have been by dwelling on totally irrational views of her situation. Of course she felt miserable and bitter and rejected, but on top of that she felt complete despair because she'd convinced herself that no one else would ever love her again and that she would be alone for ever. So she was consumed with misery about future events that would almost certainly never come to pass.

Her response to a drama in her life was to turn it into a crisis. And this is something we all have a tendency to do. We get upset over something, then we get more upset over our view of it – which is frequently quite irrational.

Here's another example – a rather different one, but just as illogical. A woman of forty-five, who's very fragile after going through a divorce, throws herself into the social whirl. She tells herself that if men want to go to bed with her, this is proof that they really like her – so she starts having lots of sex with strangers.

This story shows just how dangerous it can be when we think irrationally. If this woman keeps offering sex in the belief that any man who sleeps with her likes, loves or values her, her illogical thinking and her lack of self-esteem will contrive to leave her more lonely, used and disillusioned than ever. As if that weren't bad enough, she might well end up with some nasty social disease too.

Now you may think that your irrational thoughts never land you in such desperate trouble. But if you're someone who finds happiness elusive, the chances are that your irrational responses to everyday incidents are the chief culprits in preventing you from enjoying more reliably happy moods.

Unfortunately, our irrational views of things are often so entrenched in our thinking that they've become automatic. But in the same way as you're training yourself to notice happiness – and to treasure it, and to opt for it wherever possible – you can also train yourself to view things in a more rational way.

I'm going to give you a couple of examples of the kind of irrational views that make people unhappy – and then I'll show you how you can chart these kinds of incidents and re-evaluate them.

Dinah is a single mum with a teenage daughter. She and the daughter have a loving, but fairly turbulent relationship. Today is Dinah's birthday. Her daughter has already left for school but Dinah is confident that the girl will have left a present, or a card. Over breakfast she goes through her birthday post, only to discover that her daughter has forgotten her. She is plunged into despair.

Dinah is due to have lunch with her oldest friend at a local hotel. At first she considers cancelling, but eventually she goes – late. Her friend has ordered a chilled bottle of sparkling wine, and the food is light and delicious. But Dinah's mind isn't on the happy event, or on the fact that her friend is showing her love and care by giving her such a pleasant meal. Instead Dinah can't – or won't – stop thinking about the lack of a birthday card from her child.

By the time the girl comes home from school, Dinah is practically suicidal. She's plummeted into a self-destructive mood where she's decided that her daughter hates her. She's also convinced herself that she's a hopeless mother, and that she's made a terrible job of bringing up her daughter, and that her daughter will want nothing to do with her as she gets older and that she'll probably die friendless and alone.

The daughter arrives home from school with a big heart-shaped balloon, which has the words *World's Best Mum* written on it. She kisses her mother. Dinah bursts into tears.

The daughter apologises for not having got the balloon *before* she went to school, but she'd stayed late at school the evening before – rehearsing for the school play – and the balloon shop had been closed when she'd got to it.

'But you've got it now, Mum,' said the daughter, obviously a bit bewildered by her mother's tears and emotions.

'Yes, it's so lovely, so lovely, I don't deserve it.'

'Yes, you *do*, Mum,' said the daughter with just a hint of irritation in her voice.

I'm sure you can see that Dinah's irrational response to a situation cast a shadow over her whole day. It prevented her from enjoying her lunch. It gave her great, personal pain. She may well have upset her friend, who had gone to great lengths to provide a celebratory birthday treat, and she was so tearful and upset with her teenage daughter after school that the daughter began to feel embarrassed, unsure and slightly angry.

So Dinah spent the entire day – not the only one in her life by a long way – taking the irrational road to misery instead of considering more rational explanations, like the fact that teenagers aren't always very organised.

What torment such irrational thinking causes.

Here's another example. Julie, a twenty-eight-year-old recruitment consultant, is terrified of her boss. This is what happened recently.

One morning, Julie happened to be passing the lift just as her boss arrived for work. Julie said: 'Hello.' But the other woman looked straight through her and said nothing. For the rest of the day, Julie dwelt on this episode. She was profoundly upset by it and the more she thought about it the worse it got.

At the beginning, she felt insulted and slighted and cross, but as the hours went on, she turned the situation into a trauma. She decided that her boss was avoiding talking to her because she was working up to sacking her. She came to the conclusion that everyone in the office, except her, knew that her departure was imminent. Then her worries spiralled even further out of control as she came to the conclusion that not only did her boss not like her, but that *nobody* liked her. Then she decided that she had no friends and that life was terrible and such a struggle it really wasn't worth living.

Now Julie's plunge into despair may seem an extreme example to you, but most of us respond irrationally when certain trigger situations occur. And the resulting niggling worries can be guaranteed to explode into major emotions of self-loathing, a sense of worthlessness, misery and isolation.

Loads of us have similar work problems. And our irrational thoughts leave us feeling bruised and unwanted and incompetent. So, I'm going to make a chart (Figure 2) of Julie's encounter with her boss, and of her subsequent illogical thoughts. I suggest you look at this very carefully and that you then make your own chart every time an event sparks off irrational thinking which creates painful emotions.

Figure 2: Chart of an incident

The Incident	Your Response to it	Sum Up Your Worst Deep-Down Emotions	Rational Spin
Met my boss. Said 'hello'. She ignored me.	Miffed. Slighted. Insulted.	Felt hopeless. Felt worthless. Felt friendless.	My boss is vague. She may not have heard me.
	Pissed off. Cross.	Felt unloved. Felt life is too much of a struggle.	She's not good with people.
	She's avoiding talking to me, because she doesn't rate my work.	Felt isolated. Felt despairing.	She has loads of work pressures.
	She's thinking of sacking me.	Felt I hate myself.	She doesn't seem to like anyone much.
	I'll be out of work and never get another job that's half as good.	Felt I might as well be dead.	She obviously has her own problems.
	Also my boss doesn't like me.		She always liked my work before, so why should she change now?
	Not many people like me.		
	In fact no one likes me.		I believe I'm doing a good job.
			My boss was probably unaware of me this morning, so my thoughts have been irrational, and have caused me unnecessary misery.

As you can see from Julie's chart, it's awfully easy to start by thinking reasonably logically, but then, within minutes, to feel so distressed that you're practically suicidal.

So when a situation eats away at you all day and leaves you feeling very miserable, do make a chart like Julie's.

In the first column, you simply write down what happened. Keep this simple and unemotional.

In the second column you chart all your responses. These, like Julie's, might start off reasonably logically, but as you continue to ponder the situation you'll find that they spiral downwards into much less rational thinking.

Column three is what you fill in when you've uncovered the deep-down miserable emotions that have resulted from this one incident and your responses to it. It's not uncommon, by the way, for a person to feel really desperate emotions as a result of some event that was actually quite trivial.

Last, you look at what you've put in columns two and three and you ask yourself if there was any evidence for all the responses you felt, and any real reason for the gut-wrenching emotions you've felt. Then you fill in column four by putting a much more rational spin on what in fact happened.

When you do this charting process often enough, you begin to see what you're doing to yourself *before* you plummet into your desperate and painful moods. In this way, you re-train yourself to focus on rational explanations instead of allowing irrational thoughts to ruin your happiness.

But if you *don't* learn to analyse your responses to trigger situations, they'll continue to niggle away at you, causing untold misery.

Just remember that our thoughts often create unhappy or unwelcome moods simply because we haven't stopped to ask the important questions: Where's the evidence? Where's the evidence that no one likes me? Where's the evidence that they think I'm hopeless at my job? Where's the evidence that I am a loathsome, unlovable person?

If you can't supply the evidence, then you're being irrational. And when you're irrational, your happiness habit flies out the window.

Chapter Four Key Points:

- Our thoughts create our emotions.
- It's not *things* that upset us – it's our *view* of things.
- Seemingly trivial events can cause us intense pain when we view them irrationally.
- Re-train your thoughts – and put a more rational spin on them – by charting those upsets in life that make you unhappy.

5

Happiness Comes from Controlling Stress

The other day, I met a doctor called Rebecca. She's a GP and, like lots of other general practitioners, she feels very stressed. She told me that she can't seem to structure her work, and that she's always running late – which annoys both her patients and her fellow staff.

All in all, this very bright woman's life sounded completely chaotic. She didn't look in great shape either: she was twitchy and tense, and her nails were bitten down to the quick.

But before I could make any helpful suggestions she said something phenomenally stupid – especially for such a clever woman:

'Still – that's just how I am,' she observed. 'I'm a muddler, so I'm always going to be stressed out. There's nothing I can do about it.'

I could hardly believe my ears. Does she honestly believe that if people are stressed, they're stuck with it? Perhaps she does. Or does she simply believe that *she's* stuck with it, because she's not prepared to make any lifestyle changes?

I don't know the answer to these questions – but what I do know is that I'd love to get my hands on Rebecca's disorganised life and bring some structure and space to it. Unfortunately, she's unlikely to give me the opportunity.

You, on the other hand, are obviously keen to manage your stress, or you wouldn't be reading this chapter.

But what is stress exactly – and does it mean the same thing to you as it does to me?

Well, I think that for most people stress is a feeling that their lives are out of control. They feel that they 'just can't cope', and they're frequently unhappy and distressed as a consequence.

But just as you can do something about your levels of happiness – by taking more responsibility for them, and by acquiring 'happy' skills which you can turn into a habit – you can also do something about your levels of stress.

Rebecca doesn't believe this – and she's not even going to try to help herself. But *you* can. You can learn to manage your stress more effectively, and to achieve a more calmly balanced life – and that will help you in your quest for more happiness.

I'd like to begin by making sure that you have some understanding of what stress does to your body and your mind.

Essentially, we're all born with an instinctive 'stress' response, which is a good and important part of our make up. It's there in case we're ever in danger. And if we are, stress hormones – which cause instant mental and physical change in us – are released into our bloodstream. These hormones give us added strength and endurance, and make us feel pumped up and ready to fight. They also enable us, if need be, to run away much faster than we could normally manage. This response is often called the 'fight or flight syndrome'.

The 'fight or flight syndrome' was vital back in history when we lived in the wild and were liable to attack by people from other tribes, or by wild animals.

And even today, it can be wonderfully useful. Suppose someone tried to snatch your child away from you while you were out shopping. Your mouth would go dry, your hands would sweat, your heart would pound and you'd feel terror-stricken. But you'd probably also find yourself filled with almost superhuman strength and determination. In that moment you'd think nothing of screaming like a banshee and thumping the assailant till he let go of your dearly loved child and ran off. In such a situation your automatic response would be to fight, and with luck it would save the day.

On the other hand, you might sometimes encounter a dangerous situation – like an explosion in your street – where your instinct would send you running away as fast as possible. And your stress hormones would help you to run faster and further than you would have believed possible.

So, if this stress response is so terrific, what's the problem? Well, unfortunately, instead of just using our stress hormones in dire emergencies, we're now living in such a fast and furious world that we activate them constantly. We use them when we cross the road, or when our boss asks to see us, or when we think we're going to miss a train, or when our mother-in-law rings up, or when the cat pees in the corner of the room just when we're expecting rather smart friends!

Indeed, many of us have so much stimulus in our lives, and so little time to do everything that needs to be done, that our stress hormones have got us as fired up as a sprinter crouched and waiting for the starting-gun.

Of course athletes deal with their immense tension and their pumping hormones by running a race as fast as they can, and then by 'warming down' afterwards, and going for a meal and generally relaxing till it's time to train or run again.

But, unlike athletes, most tense people don't get the release that comes from intensive sporting action. Nor do they give their bodies and minds sufficient time and space to rest after each stress-filled moment. So their stress hormones just keep on working overtime. This is why you see so many men and women pacing around with jerky strides and jutting jaws, hollering at folk who get in their way and losing their tempers at the slightest inconvenience. It also accounts for road rage, supermarket-trolley rage and other similar syndromes.

So stress in itself isn't bad, but persistent, unresolved stress is – and in this chapter I'm going to help you to recognise what winds you up. I'm also going to help you to re-organise your life so that your stress hormones can take more of a back seat. When that happens you'll feel calmer, more in control and happier.

Of course we can't do without stress, but we also need to accept that feeling stressed is frequently a sign that we need to change some aspect or other of our lives. In that way it's similar to pain.

Pain is never pleasant, but it can be a useful warning. If it doesn't shift when we take an aspirin, we generally go to see a doctor, who may decide that we have a serious condition requiring medical attention, or possibly even surgery.

Like pain, stress should also be viewed as a warning. So if you're extremely tense and anxious, you really should try to establish what's causing these horrible sensations. It might be your job, or your parents, or your marriage, or the unhappy affair you're having. Whatever it is, the chances are that your stressful feelings are telling you to make changes.

If you don't try to sort out the source of your stress, then learning how to manage it will only do half of the job. In fact, you'll be doing the mental equivalent of sticking a Band-Aid over a suppurating boil. So, controlling your stress is a two-pronged process: it involves changing aspects of your life that are giving you grief, and also learning to manage what cannot be altered.

Nowadays, many of us think we're used to a high level of stress; we may even believe we thrive on it. But there's only so much stress we can take, and if we don't learn to control it, then it ends up controlling us. When that happens we're liable to fall victim to a whole host of physical and mental problems – and sometimes we even break down.

There are hundreds of stress symptoms. So you'd be pretty unlucky to have them all! But if you feel stressed, you'll almost certainly have some of them. They include a dry mouth, clammy hands, a racing heart and a sense of feeling as 'tight' as an overwound clockwork toy.

Then there are panic attacks, which are really horrid and which can take over your life, if you don't learn how to deal with them.

Other signs of stress include constant tiredness, migraine – which tends to occur in busy people when tension is actually lifted, like at weekends – and Irritable Bowel Syndrome, which may or may not be caused by stress, but which is definitely worsened by it.

There are also eating disorders, period pains, indigestion, frequent colds and infections, loss of libido, erectile dysfunction, a wide range of skin complaints, dizziness, tearfulness and insomnia. Then there are stress symptoms that are more to do with our behaviour than our physical state, like irritability, vagueness, an unkempt appearance, poor concentration, fidgeting and difficulty in making decisions.

On top of all of that, don't forget all the unwise things we get up to while attempting to relieve stress, like smoking and drinking. These can be as bad for our health as the stress itself.

So, stress manifests itself in masses of different symptoms. And people tend to get side-tracked by the symptoms and fail to deal with the stress itself. In fact hordes of tense patients take their symptoms along to their doctors – which, in my view, is mostly a waste of time. All it does is to clog up every surgery in the land and ensure that the country's GPs are among the most stressed of us all!

There's another problem with stress, which is that it's highly contagious.

If a boss is jumpy, irritable and worried all the time, he'll invariably have nervous, tense and anxious staff.

And if a mum is stressed out, then her family will also show signs of tension. What generally happens is that the mum's nervous state erupts into temper and shouting – and the other members of the household start communicating by shouting too. It can be a hell of a racket as everyone in the house becomes steadily louder and crosser!

If you think this sounds like your family, you can do something about it right now. Think before you shriek! Train yourself to stop before you shout, and to take a deep breath – and then to speak to your children using a low voice and a reasonable tone. It won't be easy to start with – and it won't become automatic for a while – but within days your household will begin to be a more tranquil place.

Recently, I was on a train with a young woman and her three little girls. The mum bellowed at the kids throughout the journey. She never noticed them when they were just sitting peacefully, but as soon as they stood up, or talked, or looked out of the window, or sang, or chatted to each other, she yelled at them.

By the time she left the carriage, taking her daughters and decibels with her, the rest of the passengers – who'd become tense and overwrought in this family's presence – practically wept with relief. Proof, if proof were needed, that stress is more infectious than measles!

So far in this chapter, I've concentrated on the kind of stress we get when we're too busy. I call this 'overstress'.

But you can also be stressed when you're not busy enough. I call this 'understress'. And in some ways it's just as difficult to deal with.

Understress often occurs when you're unemployed, or under-employed – for example when, for some reason, you've taken a repetitive and unstimulating job which is far too easy for you. Of course many people occasionally have to take up some kind of unsuitable employment just to pay their way through college, or to meet mounting debts. I've done many such jobs myself so I know they can be boring, but when you know the boredom won't go on for ever, you're unlikely to get too stressed out.

However, long-term unfulfilling employment is a different matter and can cause stress symptoms that are just as serious as the ones we get when we're frantically busy.

Unemployment is another huge understress for people. The day-by-day lack of structure grinds folk down. In addition, being without a job is very damaging to people's self-esteem – and of course worries about money are a real gut-wrenching source of stress.

There's another group of people who frequently suffer from understress. Nowadays, more of us than ever before are working freelance, or running small businesses. It's very rare – and lucky – in such a situation to get a steady stream of work. A much more common scenario is that of 'feast or famine', where one week you've got so much work you haven't time to sit down, and another week you're sitting by the phone, praying for it to ring and bring you something to do that will pay the rent. It's during these quiet times – when no one seems to want your stuff – that you're likely to suffer from understress.

Now, if you have understress you probably won't get the typical overstress symptoms like a racing heart and dry mouth, but you may well feel tense and irritable and headachy. You might also get a 'twitching' eye, or seem prone to colds and other infections. And often skin conditions like psoriasis and eczema will erupt as a sign of underlying anxiety.

Understress often disturbs your concentration. And motivation becomes a problem because it can seem increasingly difficult to see the point of getting on with things.

Indeed as time goes by, you might find that the less you've got to do, the less you want to do, and the less confident you feel about tackling anything.

It's quite common also to feel very diffident about pitching for work. And sometimes you'll find yourself making excuses not to do the work you actually do have.

You may also find that though you have time to go to the gym or to go swimming, you won't have the inclination. And sometimes you'll feel so bad about yourself that you won't want to discuss what's happening to you with your friends – and you'll become quite reclusive, just at the time when you really need some supportive companionship.

This understress can drift into depression if you're not careful, so it really needs to be tackled. And so does overstress. But how should you go about tackling both kinds of stress and learning to control them?

Well, personally, I don't think it solves anything to take pills. Several decades ago now, a number of pharmaceutical companies developed various 'safe' and modern tranquillisers. They came to be known as 'mother's little helpers', and vast numbers of patients were put on them. But, as with most miracle cures, there was a catch. By the late seventies, it was discovered that these 'safe' drugs weren't as safe as had been thought, and that millions of people were addicted to them. Breaking this addiction was as difficult for many patients as quitting heroin is for hard drug users.

So even if you're very, very stressed, please don't go down the tranquilliser road. To be fair, nowadays many GPs are reluctant to prescribe them, but even if your doctor does want to put you on them, they should never be regarded as a long-term solution.

Very occasionally, there may be a case for short-term use. For example if your husband suddenly died, or your partner walked out without warning, you might benefit from a *brief* course of tranquillisers to get you over the very worst days. But I do mean 'brief'. Once these pills have been in your system for more than a few weeks, it can be devilishly difficult to do without them.

Some doctors will also prescribe tranquillisers for occasional stressful situations. Suppose you have a fear of flying – and maybe you have to fly several times a year as part of your job – you might find it helpful to use a tranquilliser for each flight.

You might also be very grateful to have a small supply of tranquillisers if, for example, you're occasionally forced to give speeches, which you find terrifying.

However, chemical help can only ever *dull* your anxiety – it can't cure it. So if you want to 'bust' your stressful problems permanently, then you must learn how to *manage* them. And the first step in doing so is to keep a Stress-Busting Notebook.

A Stress-Busting Notebook is one of the most useful methods of identifying the stress in your life. You need a notebook that you can keep with you *at all times* so you can use it to record every single stressful moment that you have. You don't have to write an essay! All that's required is a sentence to describe what's happened.

I also suggest that you rate how bad each stressful moment is by putting a number of asterisks beside your brief description of the event – one asterisk means mildly stressful and five indicate you're climbing the walls with tension and frustration! The asterisk system will help you see at a glance which are the worst moments in your day.

Figure 3 is an example compiled by Cecily, who's an IT specialist and mother of two.

Figure 3: Extract from a Stress-Busting Notebook

MONDAY

** Overslept

**** Murder getting kids off to school. Had row with husband too.

* Travel to work.

**** Did supermarket shop in lunch hour – must have been mad!

*** Was then tired in important afternoon meeting. Didn't perform well. Would have been OK if hadn't done shopping.

* Got cross with daughter because she wouldn't do her homework.

** Did ironing. Had quite nice evening with husband when kids had gone to bed, but he ruined it by wanting sex last thing when I was too bloody tired.

Cecily kept her Stress-Busting Notebook for several weeks and what it showed – as it does in this sample – was that her work was not the source of most of her stress. It was her home life.

As you can see, her working day passed without much stress at all, apart from the afternoon meeting, which she admits she mucked up because she was tired after the lunchtime supermarket shop.

Of course one might argue that if Cecily didn't work full time, she'd have a less stressful home life. But she needs and likes her job; so to reduce her stress levels, she must look carefully at her house, her husband and her family.

The chances are that she could delegate more at home. Does the husband ever wake the children up and get them ready for school? Are the kids capable of doing more for themselves – perhaps for extra pocket money? Could anyone else in the family do the weekly supermarket shop?

Once she's exhausted possibilities within the family, Cecily should then work out what extra help she could afford to pay for. Somebody living nearby who needs a bit of pocket money might be delighted to take the ironing off her hands, or to get extra shopping. A solution can nearly always be found – once a stressful area has been identified.

As for the question of sex at the end of the day, perhaps Cecily and husband should allocate some special time when they can be intimate – without leaving it till bedtime, when at least one of them is likely to feel shattered.

Years ago, I read that the actress Helen Mirren always used to set her alarm clock one hour earlier than she needed to, so that she and her partner could make love before he went to work. I was most impressed. What devotion to the arts of the *boudoir*! And how admirable! Personally this wouldn't work for me, as I prefer to get all the sleep I can in the mornings! But I love this anecdote because it shows what people can do when they're determined enough to make time for important aspects of their life.

Interestingly, when people keep a Stress-Busting Notebook, they very frequently find that the areas they thought were most stressful are not as bad as other areas that they'd hardly considered a problem. Your Stress-Busting Notebook can point up all kinds of stresses in your life that you never suspected, and it can really help you to manage your tensions more effectively.

Now that you've seen a good example of how the Stress-Busting Notebook works, I'd like you to start yours. Please record your stressful moments every single day. This should become routine, until you've established which areas of your life are out of control, and have taken steps to sort them.

Your Stress-Busting Notebook will also come in handy for all those moments when you've got anxious thoughts burning them-selves into your brain while you're trying to do something else – like sleep. Whenever this happens – and it does to all of us – find a minute to write down your worries and then snap your notebook shut, telling yourself that you will stop worrying right now, but that you will return to that particular anxiety tomorrow.

When you do re-open your notebook to deal with your worry, you may well find that it's no longer bugging you.

Furthermore, as you use this technique again and again, you'll find that you can do it just as effectively with an *imaginary* notebook! I know this sounds a bit far-fetched, but many people develop this skill. So do try, because it makes life so much easier. All you do is to visualise a clean page in your notebook, then imagine the pressure of your pen on the paper as you write down your anxiety. Once you've done it, mentally snap your notebook shut and try to 'hear' the sound of it closing, then tell yourself that you are eliminating your anxiety till a more appropriate time. With practice, this technique will become second nature to you, and it's terrifically useful – especially when it's not convenient to use your real notebook, like when you're in a meeting, or driving, or when your partner is slumbering beside you and you don't want to wake him or her by putting the light on.

As I said at the beginning of this chapter, the commonest feelings that stressed people have are that:

- their lives are chaotic;
- their lives are out of control;
- they're not able to cope.

These are miserable sensations, but you can get rid of them. Your Stress-Busting Notebook will help enormously. But there's something else you can do. It takes rather more effort, but it will bring order and structure to your life, which will, in turn, help you feel more in control and therefore very much happier. It's called the Stress-Busting Timetable, and I'll show you how to lay it out in a minute.

You might remember my prize client, Katie, whom I wrote about in Chapter One? She was very unhappy when she came to me and the major factor in her misery was her stressful life. She was always late and disorganised; in fact her existence was a nightmare of running hither and thither and getting nowhere.

After much encouragement from me, she eventually agreed to do the Stress-Busting Timetable, and within weeks she had regained control of her life. She started being early for work, and also early for her appointments with me – where before she had always turned up late. And she found fresh confidence and contentment as she gradually accepted that she was in charge of her own life, and that she could affect how it went, day by day.

So the Stress-Busting Timetable is very good for 'overstressed' people, but I also want you to do it if you fall into the 'understressed' category.

As we've already discussed, when you're unemployed or under-employed the lack of structure in your life can really get you down. It's all too easy to sleep through the morning, then fail to get going in the afternoon, and end up staying up late watching TV or drinking, so that you're too tired to get up at a reasonable time the *next* morning.

Before long, you can find yourself in a vicious circle of sloth where one unstructured day melds into another – leaving you feeling stressed, miserable and horribly dissatisfied with life.

Using the Stress-Busting Timetable is the best way of breaking this destructive pattern and getting a planned shape to your days.

Earlier in the chapter I mentioned how distressing it can be to find yourself in very unfulfilling, repetitive and sedentary employment. Obviously, in that situation you can't do much about changing the structure of your working hours, but you *can* timetable your leisure periods so that you get as many physical and intellectual challenges into it as possible. For example, you could sign up for evening classes and get some strenuous exercise like running, or hill-walking, or circuit-training to counter your static work pattern. Creating this balance for yourself will diminish your stress considerably.

Now, often when I suggest the Stress-Busting Timetable to clients, they reply that they don't need to do it because they already make lists – endless lists – which they try to work through each day.

Well, lists can help – I'm a bit of a list junkie myself – but the

Stress-Busting Timetable is different. What it entails is dividing up your day and evening into one-hour segments as in Figure 4, and then planning exactly what you're going to do within them.

Figure 4: Stress-Busting Timetable (1)

MONDAY

MY PLAN Hours	WHAT ACTUALLY HAPPENED
8 a.m.	
9 a.m.	
10 a.m.	
11 a.m.	
Noon	
1 p.m.	
2 p.m.	
3 p.m.	
4 p.m.	
5 p.m.	
6 p.m.	
7 p.m.	
8 p.m.	
9 p.m.	
10 p.m.	

Each day, under the heading 'MY PLAN', you timetable what you think you're going to do. Then, at the end of each day, under the heading 'WHAT ACTUALLY HAPPENED' you fill in the *real* story! Finally, you compare the two.

This process will help you to assess where you're overcrowding your life and expecting too much of yourself – and where you're increasing your stress.

At the beginning, you'll probably find that you've forgotten to allow any time at all for some things – and that you haven't allocated sufficient time for many others.

I have to admit that when I first did the Stress-Busting Timetable, I found I hadn't planned to do any cooking or washing up at all! Since I can't afford live-in domestic staff, I'm afraid these things have to be done whether I like it or not! But because I wasn't allocating any time to them, I was always rushing to fit them in while I was supposed – according to my plan – to be doing something else.

I began to see that I'd always been like that. I'd never set aside any time to do the kind of tasks that keep a home running smoothly – and I'd built up a load of stress as a consequence.

You, on the other hand, may forget to plan other activities – like any leisure time, or phone calls to your mum or friends. Granted, these aren't perhaps as essential as cooking, but you'll have a pretty impoverished life if you never allow yourself time to do them.

By using the Stress-Busting Timetable regularly, you'll soon be able to see if you're trying to fit too many activities into your one-hour segments, and you'll start to make proper provision for all the things that you have to do day by day. You'll also find it easier to establish a balance in your life when you see in black and white what you're making time for, and what is being left out.

Let's look at an example. Susanna is twenty-nine, single, and, like an increasing number of people these days, she's trying to establish her own small business. She has teaching qualifications in ballet and tap and modern dance and she also has experience of working in a gym. So she works part-time in a dance studio, and part-time – for herself – as a personal trainer.

She came to me for help because she was finding it hard to start up on her own – and her lack of success was making her miserable. Also, she knew that she was pretty disorganised and that her lack of planning was hindering her progress. Figure 5 shows the very first page from her Stress-Busting Timetable.

Figure 5: Stress-Busting Timetable (2)

MONDAY

Hours	PLAN	WHAT ACTUALLY HAPPENED
8	Get up. Breakfast. Tidy kitchen. Bath.	Very hung over. Couldn't get up.
9	Draft ad I want to put in local paper. Go round to Claudia's. Use her computer to produce leaflets advertising my business.	Coffee. Didn't have time for ad. Got to Claudia late. She was using her own computer, so I couldn't do anything. Just drank coffee.
10	As above. Coffee with Claudia.	Achieved very little. Ought to ask Claudia to do my computer stuff for me. But can't afford to pay her.
11	Leave for dance studio. Have sandwich on train.	Left late for studio. Missed one train. The next was cancelled. Was told off at studio because I was late. Had no appetite for food.
12	Teach tap.	Late start. Felt harassed. Didn't go well.
13	Teach modern dance.	Got two bars of chocolate out of machine. Ate both. Felt sick. Class went OK. One woman said it was great.
14	Teach ballet/stretch.	OK.
15	Teach tap for beginners.	Needed cup of coffee. Boss lady looked cross when she saw me in kitchen. Late starting class.

16	Teach babes.	Fine. One of mums took pity on me and went out and bought me some bottled water. Must be more organised.
17	Go to Jo (client).	Didn't leave enough time for travel. Was bit late. Session went well.
18	Go to Di and Sue (clients).	Late here too. Session fine.
19	Have food/drink.	Popped round to Mum's because she lives near next people. Joined her for fish and chips. Bad mistake.
20	Go to Steve and Maggie (clients).	Arrived on time. What a difference this makes. Both clients doing well.

At a glance, you can see from Susanna's timetable that she was not a natural early riser! You can also see that she didn't allow sufficient time to travel from place to place. As for her diet – it was a mess. Her intentions may have been good, but instead of eating the kind of proper healthy food essential for someone as active as her, she tended to wait till she was ravenously hungry and then indulge in treats and empty calories that she later regretted eating.

You can also see from her timetable that lateness was a big problem. As well as running her own business, Susanna was working part-time for a dance studio. She wasn't very keen on this, but she needed the job to help pay her mortgage. Unfortunately, she was often so late and rushed that she was in danger of being sacked – and of course this was an added source of tension for her.

Finally, like lots of stressed people, Susanna often resorted to a drink or three in a bid to escape from her tension and the difficulties of making a living and getting organised. This drinking tended to take place late at night and it inevitably compounded her problems in the mornings.

When Susanna began her Stress-Busting Timetable, she became very disheartened for a while as she saw clearly, for the very first time, how chaotic her life was. Gradually, systematically, one day at a time, we changed her plans and her behaviour.

She decided that she would restrict her serious drinking to Friday and Saturday nights – and that if she met friends during the week, she would ask them to help her stick to two glasses of wine only.

We talked about the need to advertise her business and how this takes a lot of time and effort. She agreed that trying to fit something so important into a couple of hours when she was hung over and about to embark on a busy day was madness.

We discussed how she was going to produce really good promotional leaflets. As she'd said in her timetable, she could not do as good a job as her friend Claudia would do, but she felt that she couldn't ask Claudia to do the work for nothing and she couldn't afford to pay her to do it.

It turned out that Claudia was running a small secretarial agency from home – and she spent her whole day sitting down. So, after some discussion, Susanna offered Claudia a couple of personal exercise sessions in exchange for Claudia producing some very professional looking leaflets – and she had a deal! In fact, Claudia felt so well after the sessions that she became Susanna's most regular paying client.

So, step by step, Susanna learned to use her Stress-Busting Timetable to bring reason and order into her life. She didn't improve all in one go – there were a few setbacks along the way – but gradually she learned to prioritise, to make time for travel and eating and to be more dependable, both as a personal trainer and as the dance studio's employee.

And as she became more organised, she found that she enjoyed being organised and in control. She also started feeling much happier – and then she realised that she was drinking less, because she no longer seemed to need it.

Some months later, word has spread about her skills as a personal trainer and she's earning a reasonable living. She could even afford to give up the dance studio work, but now that she's a calmer, happier person, she's discovered that she likes the contact with the different sorts and ages of people that this particular part-time job gives her.

I'm pleased to say that Susanna is a walking testimony to the power of the Stress-Busting Timetable. It does really work – as you'll find if you give it a proper go.

So controlling your stress is all about identifying it, and also about organising each day to give adequate time for all the components of your life.

However, alongside your stress management techniques, you should also make adequate provision for some relaxation. And I'm going to close this chapter by outlining my favourite methods.

The Ten-Minute Soother

Actually – you should be doing this already! The Ten-Minute Soother was featured in Chapter Two when I asked you to do it at least once a day.

If this has slipped your memory, let me remind you that it simply entails sitting or lying down quietly for ten minutes to clear your head of clutter and fill it instead with pleasant, tranquil thoughts. You shouldn't read, or watch TV, or walk around. Just be – and let your mind drift. The Ten-Minute Soother is a great way to counter-act stress. It also clears your mind and helps you to feel good about you.

Orgasm

People don't often say this in polite company, but there are few things more relaxing in life than the aftermath of an orgasm. It doesn't cost anything, and you don't even need to do it with anyone else – so don't go having unsuitable sex with any old bod just to get rid of your tension!

The post-orgasmic phase makes you tranquil and soporific and it should also remove all the knots of tension from your head and shoulders. If you can think of a more pleasant stress buster than this, then please write and tell me about it!

Games and sports

It's a well-known fact that games, sport and exercise generally are excellent stress busters.

However, one word of caution. Though most exercise will benefit you physically, I personally think that some forms of competitive sport can be far from relaxing. It's true that after a really tough game of squash or tennis you can feel pleasantly tired and calm. But some people seem to manage to remain really tense and jumpy while they're playing – and even after a game – just because winning is so important to them.

I used to belong to a tennis club where an eminent scientist was also a member. Watching him was an object lesson in how *not* to do things.

He would turn up on the dot of 11 a.m. – he wouldn't waste a moment by coming early – and woe betide the staff if his court wasn't ready and waiting. He had to pay someone to play with him – obviously he had alienated such friends as he had long ago – and the poor unfortunate coach, who was his regular opponent, got bellowed at and berated throughout the game.

Every point was disputed and it seemed to me that this incredibly clever guy left at the end of the hour as frazzled as he'd been at the beginning. And I can tell you something else – the stress levels of everyone around him were also sky-high by the time he departed!

So if you're super competitive, you might find it more relaxing to do a spot of lone jogging, or swimming. I know that swimming can be mind-numblingly boring, but it does allow your mind to wander through all sorts of tranquil thoughts. Water definitely has a calming effect on most of us. But to enjoy real peace while you swim, you may have to find a quiet time at your local pool – like early morning. Trying to swim in a crowded pool during the school holidays with kids jumping in and splashing you is not likely to do much for your stress levels, I fear.

Hypnosis/self-hypnosis

Hypnosis, in my opinion, is the jewel in the crown of relaxation techniques. I'm a great fan. I first experienced hypnosis just seven years ago and in that first session I was taught various techniques for self-hypnosis. Since then I've gradually become a much calmer, more organised and less muddle-headed individual.

Hypnosis/self-hypnosis helps me to feel relaxed, and it also buoys me up so that I feel great about myself and confident about my future. Furthermore, it sends me off on a good night's sleep when I wake up worrying at three in the morning, and it generally cures my headaches.

Many practitioners – myself included – believe that *all* hypnosis is self-hypnosis. In other words even when someone else 'hypnotises' you – you're really doing it yourself. I certainly believe that going into the deeply relaxed altered state that we call hypnosis is a matter of choice – much like happiness!

The hypnotic state is an entirely natural one – it's not some weird kind of imposed magic. In fact most of us lapse into it several times daily. When you walk to your local post office and, having got there, you can't remember crossing the road, then you've really been in a hypnotic state: your mind has been elsewhere while your body has been working on auto-pilot.

In hypnosis, we become wonderfully and deeply relaxed; and many uptight people get amazing relief from their tension by using it.

I remember treating a very tense, miserable and angry young man. His anxiety and aggression were palpable. But he responded with great enthusiasm to hypnosis and, somewhat to my surprise, really let himself go into a deep trance. The use of hypnosis alone didn't sort all his problems out, but it most certainly gave him a break from his anxieties and he steadily became a much calmer and more balanced individual as a result. For him it worked extremely well.

Of course, hypnosis can also be used to deal with poor self-esteem, phobias, smoking and many other conditions. This is because when we're in a deeply relaxed state, our conscious mind takes a back seat and we can accept useful suggestions into our deeper levels of consciousness, where they can do more good more quickly.

But for the purposes of this chapter, just take it from me that hypnosis and self-hypnosis are excellent stress-busters.

So, can you learn to do it by yourself, or do you need to pay for a session or two with a professional?

There are people who find they can take themselves down into a deeply relaxed state. Others learn it from tapes or books. But I certainly enjoyed going to an expert for my first experience of hypnosis, and by the time I came away after an hour, I had the tools to practise it on my own.

Most qualified practitioners will agree to show you methods of self-hypnosis during that initial session – especially if you only want to use it for relaxation. There are details on getting a good practitioner in hypnosis in the directory at the end of the book.

Meditation

Meditation used to have a rather 'hippie' image, but nowadays it's a much more mainstream activity.

There are several different kinds of meditation – some of which have strong religious overtones – but the essence of meditation, like hypnosis, is to bring total relaxation to the person practising it.

Certainly the deep relaxation that can be achieved through meditation is very similar indeed to the hypnotic state.

Different methods may vary, but often meditation requires you to spend twenty minutes twice a day sitting, focusing on the present and clearing your mind by repeating a mantra – which just means a special word of your choice. The word is usually just a sound that has no particular meaning.

Personally, I don't feel comfortable meditating, but my brother and quite a number of my friends are firm believers in it. In fact my brother claims to have a resting pulse of only 48 as a result of meditation – so it's obviously working for him.

We all have to find our own routes to stress-busting – and this could very well turn out to be yours.

Massage

The first time I had a massage was at a health farm about twenty years ago – and I thought I had died and gone to heaven!

Since then it's become much more popular – in fact it's very common for couples to massage each other partly to get rid of tension in the body, and partly as a prelude to more specific sexual activity.

There are several different types of massage and several different governing bodies – please see the directory at the end of the book – but I think that word of mouth is as good a way as any of finding a masseur or masseuse who's trained, good and completely professional and trustworthy.

Massage is wonderful for ridding the body of tension, though it's not necessarily a method that heals the mind in the same way that hypnosis and meditation do.

However, it is also useful for people who are not just stressed but also unhappy. The feel and touch of someone's healing hands on your body can make you feel nurtured and cared for and result in a lift in your mood.

Aromatherapy

Aromatherapy is reputedly the fastest growing complementary therapy. It doesn't suit everyone, but it is now much more widely recognised as a stress-buster and is being used not only in health clinics and gyms but also in hospitals and hospices.

It's based on the healing properties of essential oils. But whether or not you believe that these oils can actually cure physical problems, there's little doubt that vast numbers of people enjoy the feel and fragrance of beautiful emollients on their skins, and find the practice of aromatherapy very relaxing.

Yoga

Yoga is a form of exercise which is quite demanding. It's certainly not easy to put yourself into some of the positions, but it does leave those who practise it feeling very refreshed and relaxed afterwards.

It tones up the body and helps make it more supple, but it also has a spiritual dimension, and most people who do yoga seem to me to have a sense of inner calm about them.

The late, great violinist and conductor Lord Menuhin championed yoga when most people in the West thought it was pretty cranky. But to my mind, he was a terrific advert for its powers and benefits – as he always seemed such a wonderfully decent, balanced, peace-loving and spiritual man.

If you'd like some of what he had, it could be as easy as signing up to your local yoga class – I'm not sure it'll do much for your fiddle playing however!

Chapter Five Key Points:

- You can learn to control your stress.
- Feeling in control of your stress boosts your sense of well-being and happiness.
- Don't try to treat stress *symptoms*: tackle your stress instead.
- Stress is like pain – it's a warning that all is not well in your life. Look at what you can do to eradicate the causes of your stress – then learn to manage what you cannot change.
- Reduce stress within the family by speaking more quietly.
- Learn to recognise when you're overstressed and when you're understressed.
- Don't use tranquillisers except in emergencies – and then only very short-term.
- Keep a Stress-Busting Notebook.
- Keep a Stress-Busting Timetable.
- Manage your stress with appropriate relaxation methods.

6

Happiness Comes From Having Good Self-Esteem

We use the expression 'self-esteem' very freely nowadays, but it's not an easy one to define. Some people think that self-esteem means confidence – and of course confidence comes into it – but it's rather more than that.

There are, actually, vast numbers of apparently confident individuals who have very poor self-esteem. You often find that folk in the public eye – such as pop singers or actresses – have bags of confidence in that they can get up and cavort in front of huge audiences, but deep down they have lousy self-esteem.

The most amazingly attractive and famous people can suffer in this way; and you have only to think of the late Princess of Wales and Marilyn Monroe to see that public adulation is no guarantee of self-belief.

So, self-esteem isn't quite the same thing as confidence. It isn't the same thing as happiness either, but you definitely need good self-esteem if you're to achieve a deep, quiet sense of contentment. In fact, you should regard self-esteem as an essential foundation to your happiness habit.

But if self-esteem isn't exactly happiness, or confidence, what is it?

Well, the word 'esteem' comes from a Latin word which means 'to estimate'. So, self-esteem is how you estimate yourself.

To do that you need to ask yourself certain questions:

- Do I like myself?
- Do I think I'm a good human being?
- Am I someone deserving of love?
- Do I deserve happiness?
- Do I really feel – both in my mind and deep in my guts – that I'm an OK person?

People with low self-esteem find it very hard to answer 'yes' to these questions. And their negative feelings about themselves stop them from feeling that they deserve happiness. Furthermore, they give out signals that they don't really love, like and value themselves, which makes it difficult for other people to love, like and value them too.

Now, I don't want to pretend to you that suddenly acquiring great dollops of self-esteem is easy. I'm afraid that there have been books in the past which have rather hinted that it is. They've more or less said that if you stand in front of the mirror and tell yourself you're wonderful twice daily, you'll end up as the chairman of a company!

This kind of approach is glib at best, and a load of tosh at worst.

So what is possible? Well, I'm certainly not trying to turn you into a mega mogul – though that's not to say that you can't be one. What I want for you is something much more important, but eminently achievable. I want you to develop the certain feeling that *you really matter*.

The truth is that you are a wonderful, individual and special person – and there is no one quite like you. I can prove this to you scientifically – though I'm certainly no boffin. I know that your fingerprints and your DNA are totally different from everybody else's – unless you happen to have an identical twin. This means that out of six billion people in the world, you are a one-off.

This thought might feel a bit scary to begin with, but think of it this way: nature has bothered to make you utterly unique. So isn't it time that you realised that you have something special to offer – and, most importantly, that you have every right to be on this planet?

There's been a lot of high-flown language about 'rights' in the past thirty years. For example, I recently heard a spokesperson from an infertility group declare that it was every woman's 'right' to have a baby. I'm afraid that I don't agree. Of course problems with conceiving are very sad and painful, but I don't see that we've got a 'right' to have babies. We hope to have them – sometimes we hope very, very much indeed to have them, but there's no 'right' about it.

However, I do believe very strongly that each of us living in this world – whether we're sick, handicapped, nice, nasty, rich or poor – has an absolute right to be here.

We have other rights too. Barring illness or disability, each of us has the absolute right to watch the sunset, or to hear a bird singing or to smell the summer rain.

We also have the right to make mistakes. Don't forget that 'to err is human', and most of us do much of our learning through getting things wrong before we get them right.

Furthermore, we have the right to respect ourselves – and to be respected: this is very important. And finally – and perhaps most vitally of all – we have the right to say 'yes' or 'no' for ourselves.

Many people with poor self-esteem think that they're not very important and that their views carry no weight. Is this you? If so, try to stop these destructive thoughts; because if you go around believing these things about yourself, you'll encourage other people to believe them too.

Instead, start thinking of yourself – with your individual DNA and fingerprints – as someone who has rights and opinions and ideas that are just as valid as anyone else's. This will help you to improve your 'self-estimation'.

All too often we go through life thinking not only that everyone else is better at things than we are, but that they're all perfect. However, the harsh truth is that nobody's perfect: not you, not me, not anybody. So you're on a par with everyone else. You're not perfect

– but you *are* uniquely special. And you do have basic rights. These are essential beliefs to cling on to, and they can be very comforting and affirming at difficult moments.

One way of lodging these empowering thoughts in your brain is to think them while you're doing your Ten-Minute Soother (see Chapters Two and Five).

Towards the end of your ten minutes, when you're feeling wound down and tranquil, tell yourself, very quietly but firmly, that you are a unique and special person. By doing this while you're feeling relaxed and at peace, your unconscious mind will accept this important message. And once it's absorbed it, you'll begin to find that you actually *feel* unique and special – perhaps for the first time in your life.

Another way of building self-esteem is to concentrate on your good points – much as you are, I hope, building your levels of happiness by collecting five happy moments every day.

You see, when people lack self-esteem they tend to make things worse by overlooking what they do well, while dwelling on anything they do badly.

Take Brian. He used to major on his bad points and ignore his good ones, but he's been working on his own sense of worth and he's beginning to see himself and his achievements more realistically.

Brian's in advertising and he often has to present ideas to his colleagues and bosses. He's a hugely talented and creative man, but he never used to believe it. And because he didn't believe in himself, his ideas were always being overlooked, or re-worked by other, less talented individuals.

Before he came to me, whenever he'd made a presentation to his boss and colleagues, he would slope off somewhere quietly on his own, convinced that he'd made a complete mess of it.

On one occasion, he was practically suicidal because he had a coughing fit while he was outlining some ideas, and he felt too diffident to reach past his boss for a glass of water. Such minor problems can seem huge when people lack a sense of self-worth.

I encouraged him to start writing down what he'd done well in his presentations, instead of focusing on any little hiccups.

Fortunately, this simple task totally altered how Brian viewed his work. And after some weeks of 'collecting' his good moments and properly recognising his talents, Brian started believing in himself – and his career went from strength to strength. He always had the talent, of course, but he never gave it full rein before, because of his poor self-esteem.

I asked Vicki, one of my other clients, to tell me what she liked about herself. Now, this young woman is a most charming and able person, but she looked at me blankly as if I'd asked her the world's most complicated question. So I asked her to make a list of what she *didn't* like and she filled a whole page in no time. According to her she was pessimistic, fearful, oversensitive, lazy, easily distracted, desperate to be loved – and so it went on.

That's the problem with people lacking in self-esteem: they major on their supposed faults and never give a thought to their gifts and talents.

You may recognise this as your problem, and if it is, you should tackle it in two ways. You need to identify in your head all the things that you like about yourself – this should include your good features as well as the things that you do well. And then you need to learn to feel – deep in your guts – just how marvellous it is that you have these attributes.

This exercise should help you. I want you to sit quietly and to think about the whole of your body – and to decide which bits of it please you. Then allow yourself to feel pleasure at these features. At first you'll find you're distracted by all the features that you hate, but you must banish them from your thoughts because they have no place in this exercise. Just concentrate on those parts of you that you think are great – or at least OK.

Next I want you to think about your mind. Give some consideration to what you're brightest at. Then analyse your personality and decide what you like about it. Don't rush. Once you've made your choices, let yourself feel glad and happy that there are aspects of your mind that you like.

Accomplishments come next. Select which of your accomplishments has been the hardest to achieve. Give yourself a mental pat on the back at this triumph. Then, cast your mind over all the talents you have – especially over the ones you've had to work hard to develop. Think, really think about these things – and then congratulate yourself on the skills and talents that you've developed.

Finally I want you to think about your characteristics. What is it about you that makes you proud? Is it your kindness, or your tenacity, or your intellect, or your loyalty? Perhaps you'll find several good parts of you tucked away in your thoughts that you can bring out and enjoy. I hope so. Allow yourself to feel real joy at all these characteristics – and indeed at all the good parts you've uncovered in your body, your mind and your accomplishments too.

You can take a trip round these four corners of your being – your body, your mind and personality, your achievements and your characteristics – at any time. Try doing it on the bus to work, or when you're waiting for a train. Gradually you'll come to know the real you – not just the 'you' that you've never had much time for.

You won't always want to do this, I know. As I've already mentioned, human beings with poor self-esteem would far sooner concentrate on what they do badly than on what they do well – but I'm asking you to persist, because doing this exercise will make a big difference to you.

Sometimes people say to me that they're worried that they'll become immodest or complacent if they keep thinking about their good points. Or that they'll start believing that they're much better than they are.

Of course there are individuals like that: they're usually insensitive and obnoxious, and I expect you know a few of them just as I do. But you're not one of them. Those characters never read books like this, and they don't go for counselling or therapy either – for the very simple reason that they don't want to be found out.

If you're reading this book and working at all the tasks that I've put before you then I know that you are a genuine, honest and probably quite humble individual. I also know that you're not about to get a skewed sense of your own importance. But what I hope you *will* get is an appropriate one.

Now that you're getting used to the idea that there are lots of jolly good things about you, I'd like you to list twenty-five of them on paper. I realise that this might take quite some effort. In fact I once had a client who'd only written down two good points after a whole week! But stick with it and when you've finished, pin it up on a wall somewhere.

Next comes the even harder part, I want you to add one more item to that list every day – yes, every single day of your life.

You can put down anything, so long as it's a favourable comment. You might write: 'I like the fact that I've been a good friend to Mrs Smith today.' Or you might note down something quite general like: 'I'm good at tennis.'

I was quite amazed when one of my more shy and buttoned-up clients wrote: 'I give fantastic blow-jobs.' I laughed. So did she, but she looked at me with quite a confident gaze and I could see that she suddenly felt a sense of pride in herself at her skill, and also at her ability to say it out loud.

Improving your self-esteem will make life so much easier for you: so I hope you'll really work on the tasks I've given you in this chapter thus far, because they will help you feel – in your heart and deep in your guts – that you have huge value as a person. And that sense of value will help you achieve your happiness habit.

But while you carry on working at 'feeling' your true worth, I'm now going to try to help in another way, by giving you some practical tips for standing up for yourself.

One of the areas that people with low self-esteem have greatest difficulty with is criticism – giving as well as receiving it. I'm afraid that both can be alarmingly difficult for folk with little belief in themselves. In fact some individuals are absolutely demolished by criticism, but it's something we cannot avoid.

Now, criticism is often unfair – and when it is you need some handy techniques to counter it by putting your own case succinctly and calmly. But some criticism is justified – and when we're sensible we can learn from it.

Of course it's never easy being criticised. I hate it. Who doesn't? But I do cope with it much better than I used to in my youth, when frequently I used to feel as though my world had come to an end.

Nowadays when I'm criticised, I quickly assess whether the criticism is just, or not. If it's not, I don't accept it – and I tell my critic why. But if it's fair comment then I take it on board. It still hurts sometimes, but I make myself accept it and try to make changes accordingly. I also have a little comic comforting thought up my sleeve that makes it more palatable. I think: *Yes, I did get that wrong. I regret it, and I must make sure that I do better next time.* But then I say to myself: *Still, I do have good breasts – and I do make great sandwiches!*

This is a bit of total nonsense – and it's nothing to do with anything, least of all the criticism. But it makes me smile and it keeps my thoughts in perspective.

Humour is actually a wonderfully helpful weapon in the self-esteem stakes. It certainly doesn't stop us from taking the whole issue of our value seriously, but it does stop us from taking *ourselves* too seriously.

Often when we're criticised, we're so hurt that we start excusing ourselves and rebutting what's being said without really listening to it.

A mature, self-possessed person listens to criticism without interrupting. He remains calm. If there are aspects to the criticism that he can agree with, he does so – this defuses anger on both sides. If he's not sure what's being said, he asks for clarification. If he can see that he was wrong, he says so and apologises. If he has made a mistake through not understanding some aspect of it, he admits that he hadn't fully grasped the subject. But if he disagrees with the criticism, he smiles – if possible – and says: 'I'm afraid that I don't agree with you.'

Now, it takes quite a lot of practice to feel and act this cool. So let's go through it again. When someone criticises you:

- listen – don't interrupt or start excusing yourself;
- agree – where possible;
- ask for clarification;
- when you're wrong, admit it and apologise;
- if you've misunderstood – admit it;
- if criticism is wrong or unfair say: 'I'm afraid that I don't agree with you.'

You won't get the hang of this in five minutes, but if you continue to build your feelings of self-esteem by doing the exercises earlier in this chapter and then mastering these tips to be bolder on your own behalf then you will crack it. And dealing with criticism will help you to turn your life around and find more happiness.

Now I want to look at *giving* criticism. You might be surprised to learn that this can be even more frightening for some people than receiving it. In fact some folk with poor self-esteem actually avoid promotion because they can't face the prospect of being in authority and having to criticise others.

But just as you can learn to accept criticism, you can also learn how to dish it out.

First of all, you should aim to keep calm. You should also try to make your criticism at an appropriate time, rather than waiting till you're so fed up that you're furiously angry – when you'll be bound to make a mess of it.

Take some deep breaths when you know you've got to criticise someone. Then try to say something nice before you get to the nitty-gritty. You might say: 'I think you're a wonderful present-giver and I love the fact you're so generous, but could you possibly get me perfume for my birthday instead of lacy underwear?'

This will be much more effective and will cause less distress than saying: 'For goodness sake. You always buy me scratchy, tacky underwear for my birthday. Clearly you're really buying this rubbish for you, and with sex in mind. You obviously don't know me at all – if you did you'd know that I hate wearing the stuff. You must be some kind of pervert.'

Similarly, if you have to criticise someone at work, find something nice to say first. For instance: 'Jennifer, I really admire how hard you work normally, but today your mind doesn't seem to have been on the job at all. I'm afraid I'm going to have to ask you to do these letters again.'

You might notice that people who are good and fair when they criticise, tend to use the word 'I' a lot, rather than the word 'you'. This is because the word 'I' shows you're in control and that you've thought about what you're saying. All too frequently when we're out of control we don't say anything initially, which is when we should address the problem. Instead we bottle it up till we explode. Then we use the words 'you', 'you're' and 'your' all the time – and they sound very angry and accusatory.

For example: 'You get on my nerves.' 'You're so spiteful.' 'You're bloody lazy.' 'You're sex mad.' 'Your bloody kids think I'm their slave . . .'

Try also to criticise the person's *behaviour* rather than him or her. And – by the way – this is especially important if you're a parent and you're trying to make sure that your children grow up with plenty of self-esteem. Try never to say things like: 'You're a nasty horrible little boy.' Kids remember such things and these words sink into their psyche for good. Try instead to say. 'I'm really disappointed in you. You're such a lovely little boy, but your behaviour today has been horrible.'

So just to recap, when criticising:

- use the word 'I' not the word 'you';
- keep calm and do some deep breathing;
- try to include praise in the criticism;
- try to criticise a person's behaviour rather than the person himself or herself.

These tips are just as handy when it comes to standing up for yourself in other situations. And they're very useful when you want to be able to say 'no' without feeling guilty. Just keep calm and use the word 'I'.

Guilt gets us into all sorts of trouble and it's often responsible for making us agree to things that we don't want to do. This happens to most of us from time to time. But if we have poor self-esteem it's a lot more frequent. So do remember what I told you earlier in the chapter: it is your right to say 'no' on behalf of yourself.

So when someone asks you to do something you're not very keen on, listen to your instinctive inner voice and don't get pushed into it. If your gut reaction is to say 'no', then find some way of saying it.

One way of doing this – especially when you're not feeling very brave – is to play for time. So you might say: 'I'm not sure. Probably not, but I'll think about it.'

Obviously this does mean you still have to summon up the courage to say the final 'no'. And it's not as good for you as immediately saying: 'No – I'm sorry, I won't be doing that.' But it is a start. And it's a whole lot better than finding yourself agreeing to some task that you have absolutely no interest in, or no time for.

There's another technique you need to know if you're to become more assertive. You need to learn to say 'no' without explanation. People with poor self-esteem always go into lengthy explanations in an attempt to justify themselves. Don't do this! It weakens your case. And the more you say, the more chance there is that the other person will work on your guilt and will actually manage to persuade you into the very thing you're trying to avoid.

The fact is that the reasons for your refusal are nobody's business but your own. So smile and say 'no' – and leave it at that.

Unfortunately, people who don't deal with their own needs or their grievances tend to behave quite erratically, so much so that it's not uncommon for them to alternate between being a total doormat and a crazed tiger. They simply haven't learned the mature middle way that tells the world that they have healthy self-esteem and are happy in their own skins.

Monica was just such a person. She put no value on herself but drew some confidence from being a pal of the much more successful, attractive and assertive Jenny.

One summer, they went on holiday together to Majorca. Monica thought that Jenny needed her. Jenny, on the other hand, felt she was doing Monica a big favour by having her around – because who else would put up with such a drip on holiday?

All through the vacation, Monica fetched and carried for Jenny. She brought Jenny breakfast in bed. She put sun oil on Jenny's back when they sunbathed and she was swept along with any tour or social arrangements that Jenny made. Jenny believed that Monica was having a good holiday. But Monica became increasingly resentful that Jenny decided everything. Unfortunately, however, she wasn't able to discuss her feelings in a reasonable way, so she kept them tightly bottled up.

On the plane home, fired up by free alcohol, Monica suddenly exploded. She ranted and raved that she was sick of being Jenny's slave, and that she hated Jenny, and that the holiday had been awful. In fact she had a tantrum that any two-year-old would have been proud of.

This outburst was completely out of proportion to the situation. With one toss of the head Monica had turned from being a selfless angel into an avenging fury.

As a result of her airborne tirade, Monica lost the only friend she had. She now regrets her temper, but she can still feel the frustration of the holiday. And so far she hasn't been able to understand the difference between her aggressive outburst and the calm assertive behaviour that people use when they value themselves.

Don't be a Monica. Instead, use this chapter to learn just what an important person you are. By mastering the skills within these pages you can become a happier person, and you can also develop a real sense of your own special value.

Chapter Six Key Points:

- You are unique.
- You really matter.
- You can build self-esteem by focusing on your good points.
- Identify your good points in your head, then learn to feel them.
- Learn to take criticism calmly.
- Learn to give criticism calmly and fairly.
- When making a stand about something, use the word 'I' whenever possible rather than the word 'you'.
- You have a right to say 'yes' or 'no' on your own behalf.

7

Happiness and Relationships

Can you be happy and fulfilled without being in a relationship? You certainly can.

And can you be unutterably miserable even if you're in one? Undoubtedly.

And yet most of us – no matter how modern, career-minded and independent we are – still put having a relationship right at the top of our wish list.

In this chapter I'm going to look at how you can boost your happiness whether you're currently in or outside of a relationship. Now, obviously, there are as many different relationship problems as there are people – and I can't cover them all. So in a bid to help as many readers as possible, I've picked six of the most common relationship-situations where folk need help to feel happier. These are:

(1) when you've recently been dumped;
(2) when you're getting used to life outside of a relationship;
(3) when you're in a new relationship;
(4) when you're considering marriage;

(5) when you're having an affair;

(6) when you fear your relationship is breaking up.

When you've recently been dumped

For most people, being discarded by the very person they believed was going to partner them to the grave seems like the world's worst tragedy – and if this has recently happened to you, I really do sympathise.

Being dumped hurts like hell and can leave you feeling physically ill, or injured. Worst of all, rejection tears out your heart, leaving a dull, heavy weight in its place that intermittently – and often when you least expect it – explodes into lacerating pain.

This torment makes you long for a time when life was easier, so it's common to hope and pray that your ex will return.

Indeed, you might feel that if he or she doesn't come back, no one else will ever fill that gap in your life and you'll never find love elsewhere. This is completely irrational of course, but grief skews our thinking.

So, how can you get over the pain? How can you learn to live again? How can you stop feeling unlovable and unwantable? How can you stop thinking that life has marked you out for a lifetime of solitude, misery and bad luck? And how can you start viewing your single status as a fun opportunity instead of a punishment?

Well, the first step towards a new, positive future is finally to accept that your ex-partner has gone – and won't be coming back. This means facing your sadness and allowing yourself to cry for the loss of your hopes and dreams.

I'm afraid that this is a bleak and frightening process – whether you're a young lad who's just lost his first love, or a fifty-year-old woman whose philandering husband has finally gone for good.

The essential thing to remember is that you *will* get over it. And you can help yourself to achieve that by doing your best to find happy moments among your tears, and by choosing happiness wherever possible.

Friends play an enormously important role at this stage. Earlier in the book, I stressed the need to 'be' a friend if you want to 'have' a friend. But losing a lover is one of those few times when that rule can be suspended for a while. You can – and should – lean on your pals and absorb their care and love, without having to give anything back.

Of course you can't go on like this for years! But most good mates will let you unburden your sorrowful feelings regularly for many weeks. And they'll even tolerate – if not actually welcome – the odd tearful phone call in the wee small hours.

I'm sure that you would encourage your friends to use you if they were suffering as you are, so don't be ashamed to use them. Tell them about your ex, until you have no words left to say. You'll know you're getting better when you start feeling bored! Talking is the key to recovery. When you open up about your hurt, it ceases to have power over you. Then, step by step, you find yourself looking forwards instead of back.

However, during this healing process I'm afraid that you'll often feel shattered and quite depressed, so be kind to yourself. In fact, treat yourself as though you were an invalid.

If you'd just had major surgery and were very poorly afterwards, you'd look after yourself, wouldn't you? You'd take great care of your sore body. You'd get plenty of sleep. You'd tempt yourself with favourite foods and you'd take long, scented baths – possibly by candlelight – with some background music to soothe and uplift you. You'd also allow other people to get close to you and to help by shopping for you, or taking your kids out, or driving you into the country for tea.

Well, that's exactly how I want you to care for yourself now. Your body and mind have had a shock and they're hurting. So nurture them. This is all part of the happiness habit. And, as you learned in the last chapter, a happy person is someone who appreciates and loves the real him- or herself. So, even in your pain, please value yourself and accept that you are a worthwhile and important – indeed unique – human being who has a lot of good and joyous living still to do.

After acceptance – and all the torment that goes with it – you'll emerge as someone who's ready to pick up the threads of life. But your progress will almost certainly be a bit erratic, so don't be surprised if you have quite a good day followed by one where you're deeply miserable.

When people grieve after the death of a partner, they come to realise that recovery takes the form of two steps forward and one step back. You're no different. You're grieving too. And in some ways, your grief is worse, because the object of your love rejected you in life, instead of loving you to the death.

At this stage, it's useful to see your next few months as a period of learning that will ultimately propel you into a better life.

To help you, I've devised a five-point plan. Each point starts with a letter from the word LEARN, so it's easy to remember.

L stands for List. Make a list of all the things about your ex-partner that you *didn't* like. It may start off small, but if you pin it up in the kitchen so that you see it daily, you'll be amazed at how it'll grow. Remember how he always told the same jokes? Or how she used to get drunk at parties? Or how he put you down in company? Write it all down – and start realising that maybe your lost relationship wasn't so great after all.

E is for Experience. Quite often we miss the experience of being loved more than we actually miss the person who did the loving.

Now, there is every probability you'll be loved again. Admittedly you won't ever again share exactly what you had in your last relationship. But you can have just as special feelings with someone else. This is an important fact to hold on to. *You can have similar, or even better, loving experiences with someone new.*

A stands for Appreciation. Appreciation of *you*, that is. Please look at yourself in the mirror every day and congratulate yourself on keeping going during this difficult time. And don't forget all the exercises on self-esteem in the last chapter. I know you might not feel like doing them, but they're important.

You see – often when we're dumped, we take all the blame on our own shoulders. We mentally beat ourselves up for not being more fun or better in bed. I want you to stop this destructive thinking, and I also want you to allow yourself to feel your own goodness. For example, try to recall when you've helped someone, or been kind to a stranger, or put yourself out for a neighbour. Learning to accept and value your own positive qualities is very healing.

R is for Re-organising. Unfortunately, when you've been half of a couple for a while, many of your friends will be other couples who knew you and your ex. Sadly, some of these people are probably avoiding you like the plague now, fearsome in some cranky way that having you around will make their own relationship more vulnerable to a split. But even if you keep some old friends, this is a time to make new ones – of both genders.

You might consider joining an organisation like the Ramblers' Association – many new friendships and romances grow over five-mile country walks! Evening classes are another great way of meeting new people – and nowadays there are such a variety of activities to enjoy. Try tap, or line dancing, or cooking, or computer studies or psychology, or Spanish – the list is endless.

There are also excellent organisations like Single Again. More comprehensive details of these ideas – and of other useful organisations – can be found in the directory at the end of the book.

N is the most important letter in this acronym. It stands for No sex with your ex! Often when you've been apart for several months, your ex may suddenly decide that the grass isn't greener outside the relationship after all. Or perhaps he or she will sense that you're getting your life in order and will feel jealous that you're now in a position to find someone else. Or maybe they'll just fancy a quick snog – for old times' sake.

This kind of situation often occurs when an estranged father brings his children back to the family home after a day out. Maybe Mum and Dad put the kids to bed together. Then, in a weak moment, they open a bottle of wine. Soon they're reminiscing about earlier, happier times. And – wallop! They're into the hanky-panky before at least one of them knows what's happening.

The trouble is that sex with your ex might evoke some temporary feeling of being loved and wanted, but it will leave you with more sorrow and confusion afterwards. So, don't do it.

If your ex begs to come back and try again, then you can make a decision at some later date about whether or not you'll give the relationship another go, but never have sex before this point. Anyway, the chances are that with all the work you've done on yourself, your former partner will be the very last person you want to be with!

When you're getting used to life outside of a relationship

About six months after the end of a relationship – whether you did the rejecting, or were rejected – you find yourself getting used to life as a single person. And my advice is to allow yourself another six months to pander to yourself and to enjoy some special time devoted to just you.

This is a period when you should listen to music that *you* like. And if you want to watch weepy movies in bed while eating chocolate chip cookies then you should do that too.

Maria went travelling. This was a great shock to all her friends because when she was married, Maria used to be obsessed with looking great – so much so that she always wore matching underwear! She also had a home like a palace. Nothing in her life was ever out of place. Appearances were everything.

After her husband walked out she was distraught. But gradually she got herself together and suddenly announced that she was going backpacking in the Far East.

The idea of this absolute 'princess' getting her hands dirty and her nails broken was a source of great merriment to her friends. In fact they sat around laughing as they contemplated the vision of Maria rinsing out T-shirts and knickers in a mountain stream!

Every one of them was convinced that Maria wouldn't stick travelling for five minutes. But they were wrong. She stayed away for six months and she returned a much happier and tougher person.

You might not fancy hitch-hiking in foreign parts, but if you really concentrate on doing things for you, you'll learn a vital lesson which is that you can be happy and fulfilled even though you're single.

Nowadays most of us will have quite a few different relationships during our lives, which means that we'll probably return to being single several times more before we turn up our toes. And during those single periods we should feel that we're valid individuals who are happily and actively living, as opposed to no-hopers sitting around in life's waiting-room!

I know it's easier to mope around, and to put your life 'on hold' and vaguely hope that things and people will magically happen which will solve all your problems. But the stark truth is that if you don't help yourself, but simply wait for someone else to happen by and make you happy, then happiness will elude you.

Of course it's understandable that people think a partner is the key to paradise – especially us women. After all, we've been reared on all those stories where the fair maiden finds true happiness only when her knight in shining armour appears.

The extreme case is poor old Sleeping Beauty who had her life suspended for a hundred years just to demonstrate how insignificant her existence was prior to the dashing prince cutting his way through the undergrowth to claim her!

And even today, plenty of people cherish hopes and dreams where utterly dependable heroes sweep them off their feet – and provide them with endless quantities of uncomplicated happiness.

I hope you're not thinking this way. But if you are, I'm going to ask you to abandon this fantasy right now, because it can only ever hold you back, and prevent you from putting energy into loving and changing yourself.

Instead, if you work on yourself with as much enthusiasm as you would use to greet your fictional saviour, then you'll not only enjoy more genuine happiness, but in time, you'll almost certainly attract a great real-life partner who's drawn to your energy and your completeness.

Trust me: being alone needn't be miserable – it can be great. And if we can use the time to grow and to learn to be complete, we can then retain our completeness when we get back into a relationship, instead of simply becoming someone else's shadow.

In other words, we need to be ourselves. We need to be responsible for ourselves and we need to be in charge of our own happiness. Once we achieve these goals, we can enjoy real contentment as single people, and we can also have relationships that are healthy, and that enhance our joy.

Seventy-four-year-old Liz is a good example of someone who has found greater happiness alone than she experienced in almost fifty years of marriage. And she says that if she'd known previously how content and complete it's possible to feel as a single person, she probably wouldn't have stayed married.

During her marriage she was often depressed, and she frequently felt that her husband cramped her style. She's an artistic, lively and sociable person, while her late husband was a shy man with few interests.

She told me recently how he used to resent it if she went out to her amateur dramatics club, and how, because they lived 'miles from anywhere' and she couldn't drive, she was rarely able to get out and about with friends.

After she was widowed, Liz moved from the country into a nearby town and started filling her days with art classes, music clubs and so on. She also took to dressing in very fashionably casual clothes and now – a year after her bereavement – looks twenty years younger than she is.

Liz is walking testimony to the fact that we make our own happiness. And her story shows that single people who are fulfilled are often much, much happier than people who are stuck in duff relationships.

So, please accept these three important points:

- you don't have to be in a relationship to be happy;
- you don't need to be in a relationship in order to get on with your life;
- you don't need to be in a relationship to be a valid person.

When you're in a new relationship

Couples who're newly in love aren't supposed to have any problems with happiness – they're supposed to be living in one big, rosy glow!

But the fact is that frequently when people have found 'that very special person' they feel oddly vulnerable. Indeed they experience a wide range of conflicting emotions. They often feel ecstatic, but they can also feel insecure, unworthy, jealous and heart-thumpingly anxious that everything might go pear-shaped. They can also experience a terrifying and sudden awareness of their own mortality.

This certainly happened to me. I was enormously happy when I first settled down with my husband. Every day was golden and I'd never felt so cherished or wanted. But alongside these lovely feelings came some decidedly unwelcome ones. I became acutely aware of the passing of every day. For the first time ever, I realised that I was mortal, and that my present state of happiness would almost certainly end in the death of one of us. I wasn't going around in a state of morbid gloom. Not at all. In fact I felt gloriously alive and fulfilled, but that wonderful happiness did open my eyes to the fact that one day it would almost certainly all stop.

As the days passed I learned just to 'go' with these feelings and gradually they became much less frightening. I also learned that you don't get feelings like these unless you've found the right person – and that you should be very grateful!

The fact is that being with someone you truly love removes a layer of emotional skin. If we open ourselves to great love and joy, we find ourselves equally open to hurt and grief. But that's what real living is all about. People who never allow themselves the possibility of pain can never feel huge happiness either. It's as if they go through life watching it second-hand on the telly rather than truly experiencing it.

So this sense of vulnerability is common in a new relationship. I see lots of people in my practice who are feeling this way, and they feel mightily reassured when they realise that they're not alone, and that they're not going crazy.

Another emotion that sometimes arises in a new relationship is one of anticlimax. This tends to happen when the couple are finally able to be together after much struggle and trauma.

One of my clients fell wildly in love and had an affair with the object of her passion while she was still unhappily married. After her divorce – when she and her new love had finally set up home together – she was surprised to find herself a mite depressed.

She told me, 'I'm a bit gloomy and I keep thinking: Is this *it* then? Is this what all the fuss was about?'

The truth was that she was mentally and physically exhausted, and her body and mind were just reacting to what they'd been put through. Frequently in such a situation a patient will suddenly develop panic attacks or will get a string of colds or other physical illnesses. So this is a well-known syndrome and will disappear once the sufferer accepts that he or she's tired and worn out – and then gets some rest.

Sometimes people who have left an unhappy relationship for a happy one have issues of guilt to sort out too – and a relationships counsellor can be a big help at this time.

I can't write about new relationships without mentioning jealousy. This is a natural emotion when you're adjusting to being in love with this marvellous person whom you don't yet know all that well. But unlike the feelings of anticlimax and vulnerability that tend to get better on their own, this is a characteristic that needs nipping in the bud or it will lead to unhappiness for both of you.

Having said that, I believe that a relationship without any jealousy present at all is a pretty vapid one and almost bound to fail.

It's natural and healthy to want your partner to be faithful to you. And it's entirely normal occasionally to experience a pang of fear that he or she might fancy someone else. This kind of manageable jealousy shows that you care, and that what you have is worth looking after.

But – and this is a big 'but' – there is a world of difference between the odd twinge of jealousy that shows your relationship is an important one, and the kind that can't be controlled.

Jealous people are often insecure and they tend to suffer from poor self-esteem. They also, frequently, subscribe to the very view I'm trying to wean people away from, which is that the right person will 'make' you happy. However, the worst aspect of any jealous person is that he or she rapidly becomes hell to live with.

So if you suspect that your jealousy is endangering your relationship, take the following five steps towards curbing it *now*.

- Never pick up the extension if your partner is speaking on the phone.
- Don't ring your partner at work more than twice a day.
- Don't turn up at his or her office/place of work unexpectedly during the lunch break.
- Don't sit at home moping if he or she has a weekly night out with friends – instead have your own night out and start acting more confidently.
- If your partner comes home late, count to ten – and then ten more – before voicing any accusations that have been buzzing round your brain. Instead, listen to what he or she has to say and keep calm and reasonable.

Of course I'm not suggesting you should become a complete doormat, or that you should meekly accept demeaning behaviour from your partner when there is actually a valid reason for you to be jealous.

I remember doing a programme with a woman who almost ended up in a psychiatric hospital because her husband kept insisting that her suspicions of his affair were all in her warped mind. It got to the point where she didn't know what to believe and could no longer trust her own judgment. But then, at last, she found conclusive proof that he was cheating on her. She said to me that she might have forgiven him the cheating, but she could never forgive his cruelty in implying that she was insane.

Fortunately, this is quite a rare case. Mostly jealousy is unfounded, but if you let it get out of control you will almost certainly provoke the very situation you are trying so hard to avoid, which is that your partner will leave you.

I've lost count of the number of people I've seen who've said: 'My new husband kept accusing me of having a lover, so I thought I might as well have one.'

So, learning to cope with jealousy is tremendously important. And if you can't sort yours by using the five steps above, then I would seriously suggest you get some counselling.

And if you're living with someone whose jealousy is causing problems, try to get him or her to use the five steps – or to get professional help.

While I've been writing this book, my husband and I were consultants to a BBC campaign about love and sex. And one of the questions I was asked most frequently during it was this: what is the most important ingredient for success and happiness in a relationship?

My answer to this question is one word: respect. If you don't have respect, any love that you share will fly right out of the window. When you have mutual respect you can build happiness and you can strengthen the loving bond that you share, but once respect has gone, all the other good emotions tend to follow it.

So when people in a new relationship ask me how they can keep it in good shape, I advise them to treat each other with at least the same amount of courtesy and respect as they would accord a stranger. You'd be amazed how many people treat their spouses with considerably less.

One of the problems of living together is that so often we become overfamiliar with our partner. Little things get forgotten, unless we're very careful. And words like 'please' and 'thank you' can become niceties of the past.

Unfortunately, an awful lot of couples quickly develop a habit of issuing commands to each other, which sound desperately unromantic and very bossy.

If you want to hear just how disrespectful many people are to their other halves, keep your ears open in your local supermarket. I overheard this conversation in my local Tesco last week. A young man was saying: 'Sweetheart, let me get some of these chocolate biscuits – they're your favourites.' Unfortunately, his partner was not in a romantic mood. 'No. You're always wasting money,' she snarled. 'You're a right pain.'

I caught sight of the young man's crestfallen face and I felt desperately sorry for him. I also wanted to tell his partner that you only get so many opportunities to accept gifts and compliments gracefully. If they're rebuffed too often, they dry up.

So, respect is vital in preserving a good relationship and this involves talking to your partner as if you really value him or her. It also entails respecting your partner's beliefs as well as his or her own family, space, needs and being.

I really hate to hear a man at a party shout his wife down by saying: 'No, you don't *mean* that, dear,' as if he has a monopoly on the way she thinks.

It's equally ungracious and disrespectful for a wife to stop her man in full flow in company by saying: 'Oh no – not that terrible old joke again. Everyone's heard it.' Of course she may be bored sick with it, but telling him so in public is not conducive to a respectful relationship.

I've also heard people ridicule their partner's religious beliefs in front of other folk, which I think is truly despicable.

And if you really want to keep your relationship respectful, the two of you should agree not to disagree with one another in front of anyone else. Presenting a united front is an excellent way of maintaining trust and support as well as mutual respect – and you can always sort out your differences in private later.

Another rule of thumb for preserving a good relationship is to get into the habit of good communication.

Dr Jack Dominian, a top marital psychiatrist, maintains that when a marriage ends in divorce, the reasons for the divorce can generally be traced back to the very early days of the relationship – even if the marriage staggers on for another twenty years.

So it's important to deal with minor difficulties right at the beginning of a relationship. That way you have a good chance of preventing much worse dissatisfaction or hostility later on. And the only way to deal with problems is to talk about them.

Now, I know that not everyone finds it easy to sit and have a chin-wag about their feelings. But I've managed to get a large number of my clients in new relationships to establish a half-hour weekly chat.

In this half-hour spot they talk about highlights of the week – like particularly good sex, or a generous gift, or romantic interlude – and they also discuss any difficulties or disagreements.

Now, often people say to me: 'Isn't this a bit artificial? Should you have to make time to talk to the person you love most?'

Well, we have to make time to do all sorts of things, like getting our washing done, or cooking the dinner, or taking some exercise. We don't think these things are artificial. They're just activities that we need to do. And good communication is something that we need to do too!

This weekly chat should always take place when you're sober – and you shouldn't drink any alcohol while you're doing it either.

You should also establish your own ground rules. For example:

- Both of you should fully have your say.
- Neither of you should swear, shout or raise your voice during the chat.
- Neither of you should flounce out before the end.
- You should agree to keep to time. If you both know that the upper limit is half an hour then neither of you will feel you're in for a day of nagging!

It's important that your chat takes place whether you've had a good week or a bad one. If you only have this session when you're rowing, it then becomes a big deal. Whereas if you always make time for it, you'll find that you can share really lovely moments, as well as settle any problems.

In fact, I encourage people to collect happy memories in their relationship so that they can talk about them and re-live them during their discussions. In this spirit of nurture and affirmation and mutual praise, it's then easier to introduce a less pleasant topic when necessary, without it turning into World War Three.

I usually advise couples to postpone discussing any real difficulties between them until their weekly session. This prevents those awful moments when one of you is feeling hard done by and decides to 'have it out' with the other one late at night when drinks have been drunk and things are likely to be said that will be regretted.

I've noticed with the couples I've tried to help that one partner is usually much keener to do the weekly chat than the other. But often after a few weeks, that reluctant participant is completely won over by the procedure and actually looks forward to having his or her say about matters good, bad and difficult.

One young man, not noted for his ability to express his feelings, was able to say to his live-in girlfriend that he was offended when she used expressions like 'tosser' or 'wanker'. He didn't mind if she used quite earthy expressions in bed, however! They discussed his feelings and it transpired that he had put her on such a pedestal that he felt she let herself down if she used her ripe language in public.

Initially, his partner thought he was being hopelessly old-fashioned. But the more she thought about it, the more she realised that he must have very strong feelings about her language to have expressed them. She also took on board that it was a privilege to be held in such romantic esteem by someone, and that it would be a great shame to diminish herself in his eyes through something that could be avoided.

They compromised. She carried on swearing when she was with her own friends, but was careful about what she said when he was with her. And they both continued talking dirty in bed!

For couples who really hate the thought of a weekly talking session, there is one alternative, which is to keep an open diary. This isn't as good a solution as talking to each other – especially since some kind of discussion is often the only way forward in the end – but it can provide good communication where otherwise there'd be none.

You can communicate your mutual joys or differences in an actual diary, or you can do it on email. Basically what you do is to write down good things that happen so that you can re-visit them with your partner, or say 'thankyou'. You can also write down your grouses.

Let me remind you that when you're criticising or complaining it's always a good idea to use the word 'I' instead of the word 'you'. 'I' sounds much more calm and reasonable whereas 'you' often sounds very accusing. So, you might write: 'I'd be really pleased if you could take on the supermarket shopping every week as I do most of the cleaning in the house.' This is better than writing: 'You are a complete layabout who does nothing round the house – and from now on if you don't give me a break and start doing the supermarket shopping, you can bloody well starve!'

When there are really serious gripes, like difficulties with your sex life or major issues like when you're going to have a baby, I frankly don't think the diary is the place to discuss them. You need to have such important conversations – frightening though it may be to some people – face to face.

Starting a good relationship is also a wonderful time for instigating other practices which will become habits that feed your happiness through the years. A very important one is to always kiss your partner whenever you part, or meet up again. Expressing your care for each other in this way is a very warming experience that most couples come to value a great deal.

Another good tip for preserving the joy of your early days together is to keep the image of your very first romantic meetings fresh in your mind.

Often if you're a touch out of sorts with life, or even with your partner, a bit of a trip down 'memory lane' can access those tingling feelings you had when your love was just starting. And these feelings affirm and confirm your love – and remind you of just how lucky you are.

A new relationship is one of life's major treasures and it can greatly enhance your happiness – so if you have one, look after it.

When you're considering marriage

There's an old adage about actors which goes that if you have to ask whether or not to be an actor, then you shouldn't be – the theory being that since only very few people can ever succeed in theatre, those who feel they have a *choice* about whether or not they act professionally, shouldn't bother.

I think that marriage is pretty similar. The odds of a lasting marriage are shortening all the time, so I tend to feel that if you have to ask if you should get married, then you probably shouldn't. And yet people ask the question of agony aunts and therapists all the time.

Of course, many people still have an overwhelming desire to have their big day and to actually 'be' married. So there are always going to be men and women who get spliced because they want to feel special, they want a big party and they want the status of a married person.

People also get married because they think it's time they did, or because they're pregnant, or because they want a baby, or because they're scared no one else will ever ask them, or because their marriage is arranged for them.

These relationships tend not to be overburdened with great love, romance, passion and attachment to the marital partner, but I know that some of them work, even so.

Frankly, I don't think anyone can really advise someone else to get married, but there are certain situations where I would unhesitatingly advise against it. These are:

• When one partner is far more highly sexed than the other.
This is almost always a disaster. So when a couple know that they have different sexual appetites, they'd be crazy to tie the knot in the rather forlorn hope that their disparate sex drives might somehow match up once they're wed. They won't. In fact, if anything, things will get worse and divorce will be the outcome. So if you're actively pursuing your happiness habit, avoid this situation.

• When there's an age gap of more than ten years.
Of course some marriages with a large age gap have been spectacularly successful, including the one between the late Sir Georg Solti and his wife, Valerie Pitts, where there was some twenty-five years between them.

But for every marriage of this kind that works, there are plenty that don't. So I'd caution against marrying until you're as sure as you can be that you're going to continue to find each other fun and fascinating, even when one of you is quite elderly.

• When a couple don't share any interests.
Of course many of us come into a relationship with our own hobbies, but if we're sensible we embrace at least some of those of our partner as well. I certainly became a noisy and enthusiastic convert to the mysteries of Rugby Union as a result of my man's lifelong passion for it!

I find it distinctly worrying when couples don't have any leisure interests in common – and I certainly don't feel optimistic about them staying together. At the beginning you might not mind too much that you love discos and clubs while your bloke prefers opera and bookshops, but you'll probably find it a real bore before long.

Much joy and enriched happiness can come from companionship, so to enter marriage without this vital ingredient seems like a recipe for disaster to me.

• When either partner has hit the other in anger.
Violence, like jealousy, should sound a great big warning bell in your brain. If your partner has got into such a temper that he or she has struck you before marriage, please don't delude yourself into believing that this will never happen again once you're legally joined. If your partner is contrite enough to get help, then this should be encouraged, but still don't get married until you're pretty positive that you'll never be on the end of such terrifying aggression again.

• When the relationship is going badly and you decide that marriage will fix it.
Don't do it! Marriage rarely fixes anything. If you want to give your relationship one last try, go on a romantic holiday, or take up a new joint hobby, or go for some relationship counselling. But don't get hitched – and certainly don't get pregnant either – until, or unless, things improve.

Marriage to the right person is one of life's greatest bonuses. Marriage to the wrong person is diabolical. I've done both so I know!

When you're having an affair

Affairs probably cause more broken hearts and more long-term unhappiness than any other single factor.

Unfortunately, however, they generally start off in an atmosphere of great bubbling excitement and passion – and people just don't realise what torment there is in store.

It's true that some short-term affairs aren't too painful, so long as no spouses find out. But these are the rarities.

Many affairs cause terrible distress to the individuals having them, and also harm children, marital partners, parents and even friends.

Single lovers locked in long-term affairs with married partners often ask a therapist or agony aunt if there's a chance that their liaison might end in happy marriage. There is so much heartache in that question, and it tends to be asked around Christmas time when the enquirer is facing yet another festive season alone.

Sometimes these people have been living in this weird kind of limbo for fifteen years or more. But almost invariably their wait has been in vain, because affairs that drag on for years are usually going nowhere.

And nowadays it isn't always the fairer sex who are hoping that their married lovers will leave home. With more sexual equality there are plenty of attached women intent on having fun with single guys, and these men find themselves playing the waiting game.

Unfortunately, loving someone who's not free to love you full time is likely to bring you more heartbreak than pleasure.

However, it would be quite untruthful of me to say that *all* affairs end in misery. Plainly they don't.

Many second marriages began as affairs when one or other of the parties was married to someone else. In those cases the affair was the catalyst that ended an old relationship and started a serious new one. So the end result was happy – at least for some of the people involved.

But my estimation is that for every affair that ends in a new marriage, there are probably fifty that don't. These are not great odds!

So, if you're in an affair and you dream that it will end in marriage for you and your great love, what should you do?

Well, it's quite likely that you actually know there's little chance of a happy outcome. And yet you still cling to that faint hope.

This is entirely understandable. After all, if you've put one person first for ages – even if that person also belongs to someone else – eliminating him or her from your life will cause a huge emotional draught.

On the other hand I can't tell you to be patient and that it will be OK, because that's not very likely. So my best advice is for you to ask yourself this question: *Do I want to be in this affair more than I want to be out of it?*

Don't make a snap judgment. Think about it and possibly write down the pros and cons. For example: 'I love him to bits, but I cannot take another New Year alone while he's with his family.'

When you've thoroughly assessed the situation, you can make a decision about whether or not to continue the affair.

The odds are that at this stage you'll decide to go on with it. But having asked the question and then made your decision, something significant will have changed. *You'll have taken control of the situation.*

Suddenly you'll realise that you're no longer a hopeless victim drifting through time. You're someone who has chosen to be in this adult, clandestine romance. You're a grown up, with a mind of your own, and you've made a choice to continue – for now.

Having made your choice, I hope that you'll feel freer to concentrate on all the exercises in this book. And that you'll take on board my suggestions about actively living your life rather than putting it on hold – because few people put their lives on hold more than folk who feel trapped in a hopeless affair.

But you're not trapped in the affair now, are you? You're not in it because your lover says he or she can't live without you. And you're not in it because you've got nothing else to do with your evenings. You're in it because you've opted to be there. You've taken responsibility for a very important choice – and this choice will alter the balance of power in your life.

Now that you've made your decision, I suggest that you re-ask the question every single month. That way you'll keep yourself updated about your true desires and motives – and they may change.

When Lily first asked the question about her affair with Harry, she decided that she definitely *did* want to continue with it. However, the relationship had been going on for eleven years and she had never before realised that she actually had a choice in the matter.

Posing the question made her aware that she had needs and desires – and indeed some say in her life. She began to go out more – without Harry. Little by little she got more involved with what her friends were doing in the evenings and at weekends, where before she'd sat at home in case her lover might possibly drop by. Gradually, almost without noticing, she became less and less available for Harry.

She may not have noticed, but Harry certainly did. He was used to having two women in his life dancing attendance on him, providing him with sex and tasty little suppers. They both washed his shirts too!

He wasn't keen on losing Lily, but even after eleven years he still couldn't make a decision to leave his wife. And one month, when Lily asked herself the question: 'Do I really want to be in this affair more than I want to be out of it?' she found that she didn't. And Harry finally lost her.

Lily told me subsequently that she wished she'd got out of the affair years previously. Her actual words were: 'If I'd told him to sling his hook earlier, I might have met someone else, and had the baby I always wanted. It's too late now.'

Believe me, Lily's case is not unusual – so if you're in a relatively new affair and feel convinced that your lover will leave his or her home for you, then think on.

When you fear your relationship is breaking up

It's a big step to break up a relationship at any time – even if it's well past its sell-by date. But if children are involved, the decision is infinitely harder.

Basically most experts agree that where there are kids of school age at home, parents should do everything in their power to stay together as amicably as possible for as long as possible.

Parents who don't try everything possible to save their relationship tend to end up burdened with guilt, and unable to enjoy the life that they broke up the family home for.

Now, I'm not trying to minimise the hell that people go through when they feel that they no longer love their partners. But a lot of marriages and live-in relationships aren't actually impossibly dreadful, they're just not very good – and in situations like those where children are involved, parents can frequently hold things together just long enough to give their kids a bit of extra security.

Indeed sometimes partners can agree to 'go their own way' to some extent while under the same roof. It's not an ideal solution, but it can work for a while when responsible parents – married or not – are trying hard to put their children first.

The harsh truth is that you owe it to your kids to put them first. This is what kids expect and it's their right. Kids also usually want Mum and Dad to stay together, so long as life isn't too turbulent and quarrelsome.

However, if a relationship becomes bitter and nasty and constantly argumentative, children quickly feel very insecure and separation may prove to be the right step.

Nowadays there is help for parents in the shape of conciliation, and anyone considering breaking up a family should definitely seek advice from one of the main organisations. They won't try to keep you together if it's obvious that you must part, but they will give you advice about limiting the damage to your youngsters. There's information on conciliation in the directory at the end of the book.

I've stressed repeatedly in this chapter that a relationship is not the complete answer to anyone's happiness, and that everyone should seek their own core of happiness within themselves.

By the same token then, a relationship cannot be the only reason for anyone's unhappiness. And yet people frequently make the mistake of thinking that they're fed up with their relationship, and that their partner is 'making' them unhappy, when really they're unhappy with themselves.

Such individuals frequently put themselves and their family through the trauma of divorce or separation only to discover that they still don't find contentment. Let me tell you about Barbara.

She was a fifty-two-year-old housewife whose children had recently flown the nest and she felt very dissatisfied with her marriage.

She and her husband went on an expensive holiday in the sun – the first without any of their children – and she was alarmed to find that they had nothing to say to each other. For a fortnight they sat in their lovely, romantic hotel, and ate dinner in silence. Consequently, Barbara decided that her marriage was over. At this point she came to see me.

I had to agree that the relationship didn't sound in great shape. But after delving a bit further into Barbara's activities, it seemed to me that her life was terminally boring.

Her husband had a six-figure salary and she spent her days watching television and going to coffee mornings.

Now sometimes, I guess we've all hankered after such a lifestyle, but actually to live Barbara's indolent existence year upon year would send me screaming into the sunset – and I'm sure it would do the same for most people. I told her so, and suggested she take a part-time job.

She was appalled. She had come to me in a bid to get a professional counsellor to 'give her permission' to seek a divorce. Going out to work had been the last thing on her agenda.

As we talked, I realised that because Barbara had never had to get work outside the home, she had no confidence about doing so. It was a battle to get her to agree to try, but eventually she found a voluntary job at her local charity shop.

When she arrived on her first day, the shop was in a hideous muddle. There were black plastic bin-liners full of donated clothes lying everywhere and nothing was properly displayed or priced.

Barbara was immediately in her element. She was a very organised woman, and within weeks she had transformed that shop from a dump into an attractive business where people wanted to come and spend their money.

All the skills that Barbara had honed through the years in managing a house and entertaining her husband's clients and bringing up three children turned out to be just the ticket in the shop. She became indispensable – and she liked the feeling.

Soon she looked years younger. She discovered fresh energy and made different friends from her 'coffee-mornings brigade'. Indeed her whole life took on a different perspective.

The 'new' Barbara soon had loads to say every evening over dinner with her husband. She rediscovered herself and in so doing built up her confidence and found a level of happiness she hadn't felt for years. Fortunately, her husband responded very positively to his reinvented wife and was proud that she had gone out and got herself a life.

Barbara was unhappy when she came to me and she was convinced that her relationship was to blame. But it wasn't. What was needed was not a change of partner, but changes within herself.

So if you're in a relationship that seems to be going nowhere, remember Barbara, and don't walk away from it till you're certain that it's the relationship which is driving you crazy – not boredom, personal unhappiness, or lack of self-esteem.

But what if you've come to the point in your life where you know with absolute certainty that your relationship is completely untenable? What if reading this book and doing all the recommended work has only served to convince you that your relationship is completely redundant?

I cannot, alas, wave a magic wand and make everything easy for you. I only wish I could. But if things are so bad that you avoid your partner as much as possible, and you sleep hugging the frame of the bed in the hope that not even your toes will touch his or hers, then you're going to have to find your way out of it.

Splitting up can never be easy, but the lessons you're learning about yourself in this book, and the exercises you're doing to build your happiness and to improve your rational thinking and self-esteem will help you to sort out your new life as a 'single again' person.

Over and over again I see for myself that a good relationship can augment and magnify people's happiness – but it can't provide it.

I also see that brave people who strike out on their own – having chosen single lives instead of miserable marriages – appear infinitely happier than folk trapped in the wrong relationship.

Finally, I do know, and I've seen for myself, that when people really work hard at developing themselves and finding their own happiness, they are almost always rewarded by the most wonderfully sustaining relationship of their lives.

Chapter Seven Key Points:

- You can be happy without being in a relationship.
- You can be very miserable while you're *in* a relationship.
- If you've been dumped – treat yourself with care and love. And *learn* from the situation.
- During single periods of your life accept that you're a valid individual who deserves actively to live a happy life.
- When you're in a new relationship, establish good communication and always treat each other with respect.
- Jealousy is the enemy of happy relationships and should always be tackled.
- If you have to ask other people whether you should get married – then you shouldn't!
- If you're having an affair, ask yourself regularly whether or not you really want to be in that affair more than you want to be out of it.
- If you're in a bad relationship and you have children, try to hang on in there for as long as possible.
- When you feel unhappy with your relationship, establish whether it's the relationship that's causing you grief or whether you're unhappy or bored with yourself.

8

Happiness and Sex

Why do we get so steamed up about a physical activity that consists of sticking a piece of one person into a piece of another and jiggling it about a bit?

The uncomplicated answer is that it's jolly nice. So nice that our desire to do it again and again is almost as powerful as our desire to eat. So nice that men can be persuaded into bed for a spot of hanky-panky when they'd actually planned to watch football on the telly. And so nice that empires have crumbled at the power of a penis, or the intoxicating fragrance of one particular woman's genitals.

So, sex is very nice. More than that, vast numbers of people rate it as their favourite activity and claim that they're at their happiest when they're doing it.

However – and this is an awfully big 'however' – I'm aware that it isn't important to everyone: indeed many folk prefer a cup of tea to all that humping around.

If you fall into this category, and you have no sex drive and no worries about it, then feel free to give the next few pages a miss. But if, like vast numbers of folk, you wish that your lovemaking was more exciting, easier, or more fulfilling, then please read on.

The truth is that for many people, the moment of orgasm is the nearest they ever get to a sense of sheer, straightforward joy. And this joy is one of the few sensations open to us whether we live in a fabulous castle or a Third World slum.

As for teenagers – boys especially – with their bursting hormones and their utter desperation to play 'hide the sausage', sex provides them with such powerfully intense if momentary happiness, that they'll do virtually anything to get it.

I wish I could write that women go through life with the same driving need for sex that men do. But that's not my experience. I know that many women adore sex. I know that loads of them would hate to live without it. I also know that having sex regularly is a large part of what keeps them content and fulfilled.

But I have seen the male sex drive at close quarters – not just in my personal life, but professionally. And this has led me to accept that it's a massive beast, which is absolutely central to most men's belief in themselves.

By comparison, our female sex drive is a much tamer animal; one that's more easily diverted and distracted. Most women, I think, have mixed feelings about that, but are probably grateful on the whole!

Obviously there's a reason why men have been given this almost uncontrollable drive. Imagine if procreating were about as interesting to blokes as putting up shelves? Where would the human race be then? Dead and gone – no doubt about it. So, right back at the beginning of our history, nature made sex so appealing to the average chap that he felt compelled to get off his backside, chat up women and populate the planet. He did this whether or not he personally wanted to be a dad – and not a lot's changed in some cases!

So, most men feel that having sex is vital to their well-being. In fact many guys genuinely believe that if they don't have it regularly their testicles will explode!

So what happens when they can't perform?

Well, I can assure you that most males see any interruption in their normal sexual activities as a disaster. And when a guy gets an erectile disorder, his desire to find a cure and resume intercourse takes priority over virtually everything else in his life.

My husband, who's a psychosexual specialist, treats such men, and there is no doubt that most of his patients regard sex as a major force of happiness in their lives. Many of them are quite elderly. Some of them are ill as well as old, and look as if a puff of wind would blow them away. But no matter how frail his body might be, each of these gents seems to be possessed with iron determination to get his 'favourite bit' working again. And, thanks to the magic of modern medicine, about 80 per cent of them manage it.

So, sex is hugely important to most blokes – and an awful lot of women too. When it's good it releases masses of tension and helps relaxation. And when it's performed with a loving partner it's the most wonderful, close, companionable and affirming activity on earth.

So – when it's *not* going well, we feel cheated and miserable, which is why I'm now going to explore what can be done about the most common sexual problems.

Masturbation

Masturbation is definitely *not* a problem in my view, but unfortunately people tend to see it as one.

Sometimes this is a generational thing. Through my years as an agony aunt, I've often had letters from very elderly gentlemen asking if it's 'OK' to masturbate. This was a typical example:

My wife died last year. She was 79 and I'm now 82. I miss her very much. I've been able to discuss how lonely I feel with the vicar and also with my daughters. But what I cannot tell anyone is that I also miss having sex. The physical side to our marriage was important to us right up to the end, and I feel lost without it.

I was brought up to believe that masturbation was wrong. But I need to do something with my feelings. Please advise.

Needless to say I always encourage such a correspondent to do 'what comes naturally'. It's absolutely appalling that a nice old chap like that should feel guilty, and it's even worse that the attitudes of society – even in the twenty-first century – don't help him.

When I tried to publish a letter like the one above during my time as an agony aunt on one of the tabloids, I was almost sacked on the spot. The editors had no sympathy for my elderly correspondent – instead they thought he was a 'dirty old man'. They told me that their readers only want to read about *young* people having sex.

This attitude will have to change. More and more men and women are living longer and are much healthier than ever before, and lots of them want to carry on having sex – and good luck to them.

But you don't have to be a pensioner to have hang-ups about masturbation: individuals of all ages feel uncomfortable, or guilty, about doing it.

And yet, masturbation is the safest form of sex there is. And if you happen to be between relationships it's a much better way to deal with your sexual energy than engaging in a spot of 'horizontal jogging' with an unsuitable stranger.

So if you're alone at present, I positively encourage you to masturbate – and when you do so, to take your time over it and really enjoy it. Loving yourself should not be boring or furtive any more than shared sex should. And while you're spending that time on yourself, you may very well learn new things about your own responses that will greatly enhance your pleasure when you next have a lover.

Finally, do remember that sex therapists nowadays frequently recommend masturbation as a means of helping a woman to learn to reach orgasm.

It's also useful for men who come too soon. If they can use masturbation to learn to control their impulses so that they can delay their climax, this gives them confidence when they're next with a partner.

Sexual relief – that glowing, peaceful, contentment that follows orgasm – is a very happy time for many people. And I don't believe that anyone should be denied it just because they happen to be between relationships. So if you want to masturbate – then do it. And think of it as a positive aid to your happiness.

Boredom in bed

This can happen even in the best of relationships, but it can become serious if it goes on too long. Unfortunately boredom leads to less sex, which often leads to less closeness.

But boredom can be tackled; and it should be – without delay – if it's not to lead to trouble like a sexless marriage or one or both partners seeking excitement elsewhere.

When we first date someone, there's a great deal of romance and newness surrounding our encounters. Each time we arrange to see each other, we spend the whole day of that meeting in something approaching a state of 'foreplay'. We *know* that we're going to end up being intimate together. We change the sheets in preparation! We spruce ourselves up. We focus on our joy in our new lover, and delight in the sense of heady anticipation.

The trouble is that when we settle down together, much of that newness wears off and routine takes over. Our jobs exhaust us, we commute, we have children, we have to weed the garden, or redecorate the back bedroom. In other words our busy lives make a million claims on us, and though, in theory, we're free to have sex at any time, in practice it gets squeezed out of the schedule – except for the very occasional bonk at bedtime. And then, because most of us are exhausted last thing, we tend to choose a familiar position and a reliable route to orgasm, just so we can get it over with and grab some shuteye.

After years of this, it's small wonder that couples often look back and ask: 'What happened to us? How can our love lives be so dull? And where's the passion gone that used to knock our socks off?'

Here are five tips to help you restore it – and once you've followed my ideas, try to come up with five more of your own!

- Have an occasional date with your partner where you pretend that your relationship is back in its early stages. Go to the cinema – but travel there separately and act as though you're newly in love. Sit in the back row and canoodle. Go for a pizza afterwards and do as much snogging and stroking during the meal as the restaurant will allow. Make sure that nothing can interfere with you having sex when you get home. Enjoy the build-up to it, and with luck by the time you reach home you'll be tearing each other's clothes off before you reach the bedroom.

- If you have kids, encourage them to go on sleepovers. Obviously you'll have to return the favour for other parents, but this is one modern invention that I reckon could save marriages.
- Make full use of grandparents. They're usually delighted to have grandchildren for weekends, and this means that the two of you can have a leisurely and romantic time together – with as much sex as you want.
- Have a mid-week fixture. Couples often say that they want sex to be spontaneous. The trouble is that it rarely can be – and if you wait for spontaneity, you'll probably wait for ever. So to counter this problem, put lovemaking firmly on the agenda one night mid-week, every week. There's nothing wrong with planning for intimacy. Use it or lose it – as the saying goes.
- Take a breakaway. I once polled fifty women on what one factor made them feel more ready for physical love: forty-eight of them said 'holidays'. They said that they instantly felt sexier once they left their usual routine behind.

Can't climax

An inability to climax can cause considerable unhappiness for people. If it applies to you, I hope that this section will help you. But I also want to reinforce the basic message of this book which is that no problem is so great that it should stop you from:

- enjoying happiness,
- finding happiness wherever possible,
- and choosing happiness whenever you can.

So, even while you're pursuing that elusive orgasm, please remember *not* to put your life on hold, but to get on with living your life as fully as possible in every other way. This attitude will keep you positive and will also help you to see the problem in perspective and to relax more.

Failure to have orgasms can often also be helped with good stress management, so please take particular note of all the exercises in Chapter Six.

But what else can you do? First of all, do try to accept that loads of people – including many that you'd never guess at – find it difficult, or impossible, to climax. So try not to feel too fed up or inadequate.

Let's look at the male problem first. Yes – you may be surprised to discover that this isn't exclusively a female difficulty. We all tend to think that men have an automatic right to almost instant sexual gratification, so it can come as quite a shock, both to the guy concerned and to his partners, when orgasms are in short supply.

Such a man, initially, can be quite a hit with women. Let's face it, there's hardly a woman alive who hasn't had her sexual pleasure spoiled by partners who come too quickly. So when a female finds a male lover who can last and last, leaving her to relax and find pleasure at her own pace, she can be delighted.

Unfortunately, this delight tends to evaporate for a number of reasons. Often the man becomes increasingly frustrated – and his mood takes its toll on the relationship. Sometimes the woman gets very fed up with sex sessions that go on for hours, and she becomes tired and sore. And lastly, if the couple decide to have children, the man's failure to orgasm and ejaculate becomes a serious issue.

Such a man should take heart from the fact that he has a recognisable condition – often called ejaculatory incompetence – which can be treated by a psychosexual specialist. (See the directory for more details.)

Basically, this treatment consists of the woman arousing the guy by hand and then popping him inside her at the very last moment – and it usually works very well.

Female lack of orgasm is more common. It's not so serious in that women don't need to climax to conceive, but it can cause years of mental anguish.

Often when women say they fail to climax, they mean they can't climax with a partner – male or female. But this so-called failure can very frequently be put down to the partner's inadequate technique. In other words the woman has no intrinsic problem, she's just with someone who doesn't know how to fine-tune her to a point of ecstasy.

And women often also put themselves in the 'non-orgasmic' category because they can't climax through intercourse alone – though they can manage it fine through masturbation or love-play. If this applies to you, please take it from me that the majority of women find it difficult to come during intercourse – unless they or their partner lend a helping hand! So please don't think you're a freak, or that you're frigid. You're not. You're just part of what passes for normal.

Sometimes women do have psychological hang-ups with orgasm that need a bit of help. But many females who think they're no good at climaxing can sort the problem simply by giving themselves time and permission to masturbate. They should allocate at least an hour, twice a week, when they know they're going to be warm and comfortable and – most vitally of all – undisturbed.

Nowadays there are very explicit sex education videos on mastur-bation and other sexual techniques and these can help tremendously. Sex aids too can make a huge difference – and nowadays no one should feel shy about wanting to try them. Find out where to get them from the directory.

Once a woman has learned to masturbate to a climax, she can, in time, introduce her new skills into a heterosexual or a lesbian coupling.

We tend to believe that sex should be entirely natural and that we should be born knowing how to do it, but it's really much better to think of it like learning to ride a bicycle: it's a bit of a challenge, but once mastered, it's never forgotten.

Differing sex drives

As I wrote in the previous chapter on relationships, I don't hold out much hope of a couple staying together when one of them wants far more sex than the other. And I certainly would never recommend anyone to get married, or even move in with a partner, if they know that their sex drives are poles apart.

Of course people do stay together when their sexual appetites are different, but I'm afraid that their lives together are often turbulent.

So if you're in a relationship where one of you is much keener on having sex than the other, what can you do?

Well, it is possible – though in practice it doesn't often seem to happen – for the less interested partner to accommodate the other by offering lots of cuddles and love-play to the point of orgasm. My experience is that it's very much more common for a randy man to get some sexual activity out of an unenthusiastic female partner, than it is for a horny woman to get much attention from a languid male. Frankly, I don't think women have cracked the equality question when it comes to getting more sex than their partners want to give – mostly because an unenthusiastic penis can't fake it!

In addition, large numbers of men feel threatened if their partners want to make love more than they do. This shouldn't be so in the twenty-first century, but I'm afraid that it is.

Women, on the other hand, have always been expected to provide sex whether or not the earth moved for them. In the old days this was their duty. The deal was that a woman got a man's name and a roof over her head – and he got to penetrate her whenever and wherever he chose.

But even today many women who're not keen on sex still offer it through a sense of duty. They may also do it to keep their comfortable home and status, or because they genuinely love their men and want them to have a good time in bed. And quite commonly they do it because their men are much nicer and more generous when they're getting sex regularly!

Such women tend to keep quiet about the fact that they 'lie back and think of wherever' because they fear they'll be seen as old-fashioned or politically incorrect. But their actions throw a lifeline to an ill-matched sexual relationship that would never otherwise survive.

Sometimes couples with different levels of desire are able to stay together by scheduling their sex sessions. For some reason, if the highly sexed partner really knows when he or she is next going to be able to make love, then the arguments stop and both parties can relax and get on with the rest of their lives. As for their partners, even people who quite dislike sex are often able to face it on, say, Wednesdays and Saturdays, if they know that they'll be left alone on the other days! And the randier half of the couple can always masturbate when intercourse is not on the timetable.

Another way that ill-matched couples manage to stay together is when the person with the bigger sex drive goes elsewhere for satisfaction.

I can't recommend this. Affairs might start as an uncomplicated exercise for the genitals, but people's hearts usually get involved – or broken – before long. And obviously there are all kinds of risks to people's self-esteem, health and security when they go to prostitutes.

Still – these things do go on, and there's no doubt that some couples keep their act together by one of them turning a blind eye to the extra-curricular sexual antics of the other.

So far I've been writing about differing sex drives in the long term. But sometimes couples find that their desires are out of kilter for a shorter period.

A typical example is when a man with a colossal sex drive meets up with an inexperienced woman. At first their needs may seem to be very different, but once she gets into her sexual stride, she may quickly become as enthusiastic as her more practised lover.

Then there are times in many good and well-matched sexual pairings when one partner is temporarily less interested than the other. When this occurs, it's perfectly possible that with careful handling, sex – and indeed the broader relationship – can survive.

Among the most common reasons for one partner going off sex is the birth of the baby. Strangely, this can occasionally be the guy. Sometimes he can be so overwhelmed with the responsibility of becoming a parent that sex takes a back seat for a while.

Rather more commonly, men are upset at the sight of their partner in pain while giving birth – and this can make monks of them for ages. I'm afraid that sometimes this loss of libido can be serious and long lasting. So, if any pregnant woman reading this is currently endeavouring to persuade her man – against his will – to watch the birth of their child, I'd advise her to think again. It might be better to have your mum, friend or sister with you rather than risk ruining an important part of your relationship.

Most men, however, want sex to get going again as soon as possible after the birth. Unfortunately, vast numbers of women don't – especially those who've had vaginal deliveries.

This is such a difficult time – and just when the young parents thought they were going to be extra happy and fulfilled with their new child.

Such a couple need cartloads of patience with each other. The woman needs to feel that the man is not just being difficult in wanting her body – which she wants to reserve for maternal purposes. And the man needs to accept that he's not being forced out of his own home and bed, and to understand that his partner requires a break from being a sex siren while she adjusts to motherhood.

Ideally, such parents should get someone else to look after their babe on a regular basis so that they can have time together to recapture what it felt like to be just a couple.

Relatives and friends are always asking what they can do when there's a baby in the house. Well this is it! Giving the new mum and dad a bit of a breather is the best help imaginable. When a couple can talk in private and hug and just 'be', the whole thorny issue of intimacy will generally begin to resolve itself.

It won't happen overnight, but if a new mum can agree to help her partner to achieve sexual satisfaction by a method that suits them both, then he'll be a lot happier and easier to live with.

And if the young dad will try to forget his pride and his penis just temporarily, and will cuddle and love his partner – and not get stroppy if she won't give him full sex – then he'll be rewarded with gratitude and love for his maturity and support.

This is a crucial time in any sexual relationship – and it's really important that a temporary imbalance in sexual desire should not drive a wedge between two loving people who were previously enchanted with each other.

I usually advise such a couple to find a code word that means 'I'm not up for sex but I could really use the biggest hug in the world.'

This does at least ensure lots of physical closeness. It also prevents that awful situation where the mum won't instigate any physical contact in case it leads to unwanted sex, and the dad won't stretch out a loving hand in case his partner misinterprets the action as a demand for intercourse.

In this situation the couple can end up hardly touching at all, just when they both need masses of love and reassurance.

Having a new baby should be a wonderfully happy time, but all too often it's the most difficult period in a relationship. So keep touching, and keep remembering to be aware of all those factors in your spouse that attracted you to him or her in the first place. And as time passes, your sex drives should settle down into their old pattern.

Erectile dysfunction

There is absolutely no doubt that erectile dysfunction – that's the new name for impotence – is a condition that knocks happiness on the head for the vast majority of men who suffer from it.

I watch guys with this problem when they come to see my husband at our clinic, and it's obvious that they're extremely fed up with the situation.

But fortunately, now that we have Viagra and other effective treatments, the great majority of impotent men can resume their sex lives. And I can bear witness to the vast difference in such men once the pills have taken effect.

On their first visit to our clinic they are, not surprisingly, quite nervous. They also seem depressed, and as if they're carrying a great weight on their shoulders.

On the next visit – once they've had a good result and have managed to make love to their partners – they've got a spring in their step, a smile playing around their lips and a definite sparkle in their eyes. It doesn't matter whether they're twenty or eighty – as some of our patients are – they're thrilled to bits.

So I know how important sex is to most men because I see the difference in them when they can do it again – sometimes after years of problems. And I can feel the joy and satisfaction that bursts from them.

So, treatments for erectile dysfunction definitely contribute to people's happiness, and we can't ignore the fact that new lifestyle drugs, like Viagra, are playing a huge part in improving the quality of people's existences.

Certainly, I'm convinced that sex is a vital ingredient in most folk's menu of contentment, so I urge any man with potency problems to see a doctor to find out how he can best be helped.

Premature ejaculation

I've never been on a radio or television programme about sex without someone ringing in about premature ejaculation, or PE. It is phenomenally common and it causes anxiety and misery in masses of relationships.

Men feel hopeless and depressed that they can't satisfy their lover, and women often just give up on sex because they're fed up with a situation where their guy always climaxes before they even get going.

But the really good news is that PE can be cured quite quickly in most cases. Unfortunately however, most people don't go and get the help that's available.

The best and the most tried and tested cure for PE is the famous Masters and Johnson grip. Sounds painful! But it isn't.

This grip was devised by the renowned American sex researchers over twenty-five years ago, and they claimed it cured 98 per cent of PE cases.

It's a simple technique, which can be quickly taught by an expert, and it involves the woman grasping the male organ in a particular way every time the man approaches his 'point of no return'.

Within weeks, the man can usually keep going for much longer than he could before, so that the couple can enjoy more satisfying sex. So if you or your partner are having trouble in this area, please consider getting help at a psychosexual clinic. (See the directory for details.)

A small number of doctors prefer to treat PE with an anti-depressant called clomipramine. If you're interested in this method please see your GP. But do remember that all anti-depressants are powerful drugs and they all have side-effects, so you need to take that fact into consideration.

You might remember an earlier chapter in this book where I urged you to put right what you can, and accept what you can't. *Don't* accept PE. This is something that can be put right – and you'll feel much happier if you do.

Selfishness

Living with a sexually selfish partner is a major sex problem. But since you can't really go to your doctor about it, or pop a pill, I'm afraid people often just put up with it – feeling unhappier with every passing year.

To be fair, lovers are often selfish through ignorance rather than through unkindness. Many a man, for example, goes through life believing that simple sexual intercourse – taking his weight on his elbows, of course – is all that's required of him as a gentleman.

But if you're a woman on the receiving end of a guy who thinks that humping away with no love-play before or after is quite sufficient, you'll probably end up deeply frustrated and angry.

Such poor performers can be pitied and even forgiven initially. But it's a very different story if you show a man that you want something different and he refuses to mend his ways. When that happens, he crosses the fine line between ignorance and intentional selfishness – and there are few conditions more depressing to live with than that.

In a book I wrote with my husband called *The Big 'O'*, I coined the phrase 'Roll On, Roll Off Romeos' to describe such inadequate lovers.

That was five years ago, but there are still plenty of them about. You'll know if you've ever been with one. This is a guy who thinks his hands are for grasping your upper arms, breasts and buttocks. He hasn't a clue that he should be twiddling those other bits that send you soaring into outer space.

If you're hitched to such a gent, make sure he reads this chapter. I also suggest you supply him with some sex-education videos and books.

In addition, do explain that your clitoris is the equivalent of his penis – and spell out to him that this is the bit of you that would have grown into a todger if you'd developed into a baby boy in the womb, instead of a girl.

Next, show him exactly what your clitoris looks like so that he can see for himself how it resembles the male organ. Then ask him how he'd like to have sex without his penis being touched, stroked and stimulated. Get him thinking about this – because even today there are men who believe that a woman should climax with no difficulty if a guy does nothing but pump away at her vagina.

I'm afraid that not all male partners respond well to this kind of love lesson. A friend of mine tried to show her 'hands free' lover where she wanted to be touched by placing his fingers right on the critical spot. He recoiled as if he'd been scalded and uttered the immortal words:

'That doesn't do much for me, babe.'

Thank God she chucked him. And if you've got a bloke like him, he should probably go the same way. Life's too short to stay shackled to a selfish lover – because they're never just selfish in bed, they're horrendous out of it too.

There's only one way you can survive with a sexually selfish man and that is to creep out to the bathroom once he's 'had' you and masturbate. There are women the world over doing that. In a previous time, and with a previous partner, I was one of them – and it was pretty demoralising.

Mind you, I wouldn't want to suggest for a second that selfishness is a male-only preserve. Not at all.

There are plenty of women who won't do things in bed that their partner longs for – like hand stimulation, or oral sex. There are females who make sure that they get their own orgasm from their partner and then ignore his needs or snap: 'Oh, do hurry up and get it over with.'

And there are very definitely women who act sexy when they want something – like a new baby or a holiday in the sun – and then refuse all sex at other times. This can be soul-destroying for a man.

Selfishness in either gender is unkind and unsexy – and tolerating such behaviour will damage your self-esteem and hinder your quest for happiness.

Vaginismus

If you're a woman who has never had intercourse, and who dreads the thought of penetration, and who also contrives to avoid smear tests and has never worn internal sanitary protection, then it's quite likely you have a condition called vaginismus.

This is not your fault – and you're not being intentionally difficult or prudish. But for some reason, your vaginal muscles – and maybe even your thighs too – clamp together whenever intercourse is a possibility, and stop it happening.

Women who suffer in this way often had strict upbringings where they were given very unhelpful messages like: 'all men are beasts' or 'sex is painful' or 'sex is dirty' or that 'nice girls don't'.

Sometimes this state of affairs can go on for years. And there are definitely a significant number of unconsummated marriages where vaginismus is such a problem that the female partner remains a virgin for decades.

Indeed many women only seek help for this problem when they want to become mothers.

By the way, if you have vaginismus it doesn't necessarily mean that you hate sex or that you have no desire. The reverse may be true and you may enjoy petting or masturbation to orgasm – so long as your vagina is left strictly alone.

There is good medical/behavioural treatment available for this condition and if you want to know more do go along to your doctor.

This has been a quick run around the most common sex problems that cause people pain and misery. As you'll have noticed, many of them can be quickly remedied, so I hope you'll take action to put right any problems you may have.

Sex, and especially the moment of orgasm, can greatly enhance our happiness. And I believe that we should collect and treasure our sexual memories unashamedly – like all of life's great and exciting moments. So if sex is an important part of your happiness profile then make it as good as possible – and enjoy it.

Chapter Eight Key Points:

- Good sex releases tension and helps relaxation.
- Sex with a loving partner is a close, companionable and affirming activity.
- Masturbation is good for you – and is a very safe form of sex.
- Don't let boredom in bed ruin your sex life or your love. Tackle it!
- Ejaculatory incompetence, premature ejaculation and erectile dysfunction (impotence) can all be treated very satisfactorily these days.
- Women can learn to climax through masturbation and by using sex education videos and sex aids.
- Ill-matched sex drives can prove disastrous for a couple, but with compromise relationships can be saved.
- Selfish lovers will damage your self-esteem and hinder your happiness habit.
- If you like sex, make it part of your happiness profile and enjoy it.

9

Happiness Comes from Understanding What Kind of Parenting You Had

Did your parents shower you with love when you were a child?

Did they constantly boost your confidence by telling you that you looked great and that you were good at things?

Were they careful never to refer to *you* as 'bad' or 'disgusting' – even if they had to take issue with your behaviour?

And when they had to reprimand you, did they do it in such a way that you were in no doubt that they still really, really loved you?

If your answer is 'yes' to all of these questions, then BE VERY, VERY GRATEFUL!

And if now, as an adult, you still feel their affirmation and you can discuss most things with them and feel happy in their company – even though you're pleased to have your own independence and life of your own – then you are fortunate indeed!

It's more likely, alas, that your upbringing was far less perfect. Maybe your mum and dad, for whatever reason, were just not very good at being parents. If this is so, you're certainly not alone. Vast numbers of adults, who are currently struggling with their levels of happiness, have been seriously short-changed in the parenting stakes. And for them Philip Larkin's most quoted line, 'They fuck you up, your mum and dad . . .', is too close to the truth for comfort.

The other day, an eminent woman writer told me that she'd never have psychotherapy because 'all it does is blame parents for your problems'. Well, I don't apportion blame in my consulting room and I have no intention of doing so in this book either – for a start there's absolutely no point in deciding that our problems are the 'fault' of any particular person, since it does nothing to solve them. However, I *do* think it's useful to look at what parents should provide, and also at how we feel when this doesn't happen.

Now, you may feel uneasy about looking too closely at your own family. You may worry that by digging up all that ancient stuff you'll make things worse, or that you'll feel unhappier, not better.

However, my experience is that if we know what we're dealing with, then coping with it becomes easier.

Many unhappy people feel a whole mixture of feelings for their parents which they cannot understand. Sometimes they feel a deep sense of longing. Often they feel disappointment. Frequently they suddenly feel very hostile to the people who brought them up. In other words, confusion reigns.

By looking at the reality of our parents, we can finally allow ourselves to see them as they are. Sometimes it's a great weight off someone's mind and shoulders to be able to say about their father: 'He was a charming man, but a waste of space as a dad.' Or about their mother: 'Hilarious woman – lousy mum.'

Getting an accurate picture of their parents enables people to experience their 'true' feelings, as opposed to the ones they believe they 'ought' to have.

'Ought' is a word that crops up rather a lot in families. I 'ought' to love my father more. I 'ought' to have mother to stay now she's old. 'Ought' covers a multitude of conflicts, and using it only puts pressure on yourself. So try never to say it.

I've said elsewhere in the book that when an unhappy person

comes for therapy, it's common to feel the palpable presence of one or other of that client's parents in the room with you.

I must also say that I have yet to treat an unhappy person, or someone who is lacking in self-esteem or confidence, who has had really positive parenting.

So this chapter is for everyone who knows that some of their current unhappiness stems from what was done, or not done, by their parents. It's not easy to talk about such things, or to face up to them, but I have seen too many sad people damaged by their parents to be inhibited about bringing these issues into the open. And I can only ask you to bear with me if you're one of those rare folk whose childhood was so golden they wouldn't have changed any of it.

A quick word here for any readers whose childhood difficulties went beyond the kind of problems that are highlighted in this chapter – people who were seriously deprived or who suffered long-term sexual abuse. Much of what I have to say will benefit you, but it may not go far enough. The directory at the end of the book will point you towards further appropriate help.

Very many folk who feel that their experience of parenting was lacking in some way actually had the kind of home life that appeared fine from the outside. What went on indoors was unfortunately a different matter.

One of my clients, who was badly neglected by her mother, told me that outside the family home her parent was a tireless charity worker and regarded by most people as a saint! Indoors, however, she was rather more of a sinner, since she never had time for her kids.

Now, I'd be the first to admit that most mothers and fathers do their best – or think that they do. I also acknowledge that all parents are a product of their own parenting, which may have been pretty dire in some cases. Still, the buck has to stop somewhere.

The tough truth is that when someone becomes a parent, he or she joins a new and very important club. And the rules of that club are that from the moment of a child's birth, parents should willingly do everything necessary to care for their new infant – emotionally and physically. It's an onerous task, no doubt about it; but for about the next eighteen years, they must put their child's needs at the very top of their list of priorities. That is what they're there for. That's their job.

Think of the birds in your garden. They devote their whole existence to building a nest, nurturing their eggs and then feeding their babies and teaching them to fly. They are totally absorbed in their offspring. They put them first. That's what they're programmed to do. And if they can do it – so, I feel, should we.

So our parents must take full responsibility for our physical well-being and our emotional development as children. And ultimately they must also take the lion's share of responsibility for how our relationship with them turns out. They were on this planet first, after all.

Some parents, sadly, aren't very good at shaping our emotional development, or at forging a good relationship with us, because they don't give us enough authentic, genuine and selfless loving.

Some parents in fact are too needy themselves to give love, and as their offspring grow they contrive all sorts of ways to persuade their children to mother them.

Some parents, on the other hand, can be very loving but then, if the child misbehaves or doesn't agree with them, quickly become cold and distant.

Some parents are totally self-obsessed. Others are absent.

I'm not saying that all these inadequacies are the 'fault' of the parents: who knows what these people may have gone through themselves? And I'm not saying they're to blame. But I am saying they're accountable.

I'm also saying – and I realise that some people will think this is harsh or controversial – that these parents only have a right to reap what they sowed. In other words they can only expect to receive the sort of love that they gave out.

So if your parents showed you great love and warmth and respect, the chances are that you feel love, warmth and respect for your parents. But if they didn't give you those things, then you probably feel that something is wrong with your relationship with them. You may well wish that you could love them more – in a joyful and uncomplicated sort of way – but find that in reality such positive emotions are absent.

If this is how you feel, it may help you to recognise that your parents haven't actually earned the right to receive much love, warmth and respect from you, because, for their own reasons, they didn't deliver it.

Think of it this way. You have an emotional bank inside you. It's somewhere deep in your guts behind your diaphragm: this is where you feel your basic, innermost feelings.

When we're children, we are totally dependent on our parents paying into our emotional bank: there's no one else to do it. So when we reach adulthood there should be a substantial amount in it. When that happens, we can 'pay out' love to our friends and partners – and to our parents too. But if there's not much in our emotional bank, we can seem too miserly with our emotions, or rather anxious about sparing or sharing our love.

Thankfully that's not the end of the story. Plenty of people who had emotionally impoverished childhoods make up their minds to be totally different in character from their parents – and they work really hard to make the necessary changes.

Some labour alone, others read books like this one, a few have therapy and a growing number attend self-assertiveness classes. Whatever method they use, they generally emerge as stronger and much more loving individuals than their parents were. But it's very hard work for them. And it wouldn't have been nearly so difficult if their parents had topped up their emotional savings account more frequently.

Clients often come to me at a time when their parents are becoming more elderly and demanding. In a nutshell, these clients are facing an emotional crisis because they're being expected to deliver more love and care *to* their parents than they ever got *from* them.

I work with my clients and help them to reappraise just how much nurture, love and attention they had as children. Often the client feels deeply saddened as he or she faces, perhaps for the first time, the harsh truth that they were never loved very much.

But having uncovered that and revisited it, they generally become stronger. And in their new-found strength, they are able to examine their emotional bank account and to ascertain just how much was paid into it by their parents. Once they've completed these calculations, they feel much freer and able to decide how much it's appropriate to repay.

This moment of assessment and accountability needn't be hostile. Frequently, having delved back into their childhood and seen clearly for the first time just what sort of people their parents were and are, these adult 'children' become amazingly accepting of them. Sometimes, indeed, the relationship between parent and offspring becomes more affectionate and workable than it's ever been before.

Earlier in the book I said that happiness comes from putting right what you can in life, and accepting what you can't. That is certainly true of parents.

You can't 'put right' how much they paid into your emotional bank account any more than you can put right their behaviour and attitudes. Neither can you magically transform them into the sort of mum and dad that you'd like to have had. Nor can you alter what they did to you in the past. But what you can do is to 'accept' the reality of how it was.

In the rest of this chapter, I'm going to describe different types of flawed parenting. They may not be identical to your own but they should help you to uncover and accept the reality of your own parents. Once you've done that, you'll find you're in a position to make some choices about them.

You might choose to treasure the good times you've had with them. You might choose to allow yourself to feel such love as they've been able to give you. You might choose to accept their shortcomings and to see more of them. Or you might choose not to have any contact at all.

There are, actually, masses of choices about family relationships – but often we refuse to see them. Once you've read the following character studies of flawed parents, you should be able to see your options more clearly.

The self-obsessed parent

'Not now, darling – Mummy's busy.' These five words are the anthem of the self-obsessed parent, who is almost always female.

What the SOP likes best is concentrating on herself and talking about herself – and so long as her children go along with that, everyone gets on fine.

The SOP gets lots of headaches – especially at weekends when she might otherwise be free to give some attention to her offspring. So, from a very early age, her children learn to be very quiet and undemanding. They hope that being 'good' children will bring them her approval. This rarely happens, but at least by being 'invisible' they don't incur her wrath, which can be horrible to witness.

The SOPs are often, though not invariably, career women. So their justification for not giving time to their kids is that they're working for a better future for them.

In truth, the SOP works hard because of her own ambition and drive. She is principally interested in developing herself rather than turning out brilliant children who might outshine her.

The SOP can be quite generous with presents, as in 'There, if mummy just stayed at home and talked to you, she wouldn't be able to buy you this fabulous pony...'

But her present-giving is usually done to appease any guilt she feels – and woe betide the child who doesn't fall over herself with gratitude.

The SOP is often a good provider, but she chooses *what* to provide in terms of her own status. If there's the slightest criticism of her as a mother, she'll immediately justify herself by saying: 'But, darling, what more could I have done? I did send you to the very best boarding school...'

Of course the chances are that her poor child didn't want to go to that school anyway and was only sent there because of Mum's social ambitions.

As the child of an SOP, you're supposed to be admiring of her at all times, and very grateful. The SOP thinks that your life is perfect, just because you're her child, so if you dare to suggest you'd like to talk about any problems you've got she'll say: 'But you have everything, sweetie. What little worries could you possibly have? If you want to know about problems, I'm the one who's got problems . . .'

If you flunk your university exams, or your relationship fails, she will take the news as a personal insult and will tell you how selfish you are to cause her this worry when her nerves are already shot to pieces.

Other people frequently think the SOP is terrific. Indeed her friends think she's so great that they frequently pity her for having such dull offspring, little knowing that she has cowed her kids into submission.

So what can you do as an adult to deal with this SOP? Well, it's pointless expecting her to change. So you have to accept her.

I have a client who's in her late fifties. All her life, her mother has taken centre stage and all her life, my client has waited for her mother to notice her and put her first. She's still waiting.

Sadly, all you can do with the SOP is to laugh with and at her. Don't keep trying to please her, because you can't.

Nicky – the daughter of an SOP – came to me when she was about to get married. She knew she should be happy but she couldn't stop crying, and she couldn't understand her feelings.

Her fiancé was tall, American, wealthy, well-connected and charming: a 'designer' boyfriend, in fact!

Nicky's mother was American too – and a social climber – and everything about Nicky's fiancé delighted her.

As Nicky described her relationship with her man to me, she wept copiously into a box of man-size tissues. Her grief was acutely painful to witness and I could find no way to console her until I suggested that she postpone her wedding. This at least gave her breathing space and the tears stopped.

At our next meeting she told me that she'd realised that she had picked a partner to please her mother, not herself.

'All my life I've tried to do the right thing for her,' she whimpered. 'As a child I tried so hard not to mind that she never had time for me – perhaps I thought that she would love me more if I married well . . .'

Nicky spent several sessions with me crying the tears that had been saved up for years and years and years. She talked about her childhood and uncovered a whole history of emotional neglect. It was a painful shock for her to see the reality of her self-obsessed parent fully for the first time, but once she had seen and accepted it, she set herself free.

Before long, she gave up the designer boyfriend – even though it sent her mother to bed with a migraine for a week. And soon afterwards she met a lad who was wacky, and kind and interesting and creative, and not at all the man her mother would have chosen. She had a narrow escape.

So if your mother is an SOP, put yourself first for a change. After years of playing second fiddle to her, it's time you did.

As for the future with your SOP, you must do what feels right. If you choose to be kind to your mother and to indulge her when you meet, then you'll not only keep the peace but you'll have the benefit of knowing that you're a much nicer person than she ever was. But it may be that facing how she is will make you decide to keep your distance from now on.

Whatever you decide, don't put your SOP's needs before yours ever again. Instead, value yourself and share all the love you've got inside you with other people who are more deserving of you, and who have the emotional capacity to love you back.

Frequently, people with SOPs develop a stronger relationship with their other parent once they've stopped trying to please the SOP and have found a new perspective for her.

And many children of SOPs forge great relationships with their mums-in-law, finding a substitute and belated kind of mother-love from them.

Having an SOP doesn't give you a great start in life. But you can get over it by facing up to the frailties of your parent, and then making sure that you put yourself first in the future.

Certainly as your SOP gets older, there'll be all sorts of pressure from her or her friends for you to do more for her. But just remember the birds in the garden. They're much better parents than your SOP ever was, and yet they have no expectation of their babies coming back and looking after them in their dotage! That's not nature's way.

What is important from now on is that you have a loving life of your own, and that you allocate time to your SOP according to what you feel is appropriate, and not according to other people's views, or the hysterical demands of your parent.

The emotionally stunted parent

This kind of parent can be male or female. Often emotionally stunted people marry each other, so you're likely to have a brace of ESPs.

A favourite phrase of ESPs is: 'We won't stand in your way', which basically means that they're too timid or withdrawn actually to help you. And because ESPs find shows of emotion or personality very difficult, another familiar phrase is: 'Don't show me up.' They usually deliver these words as a snarl out of the corner of their mouths and use them whenever you're doing anything that might occasion some notice.

A friend of mine remembers that as a child she went with her ESPs to a pantomime. During the show she noticed a little girl in the row in front. This child was leaning against her daddy with her head on his shoulder. My friend wondered what it would feel like to get that close to her own father. Tentatively, she laid her own head on his shoulder. He shrugged her off and hissed: 'I hope you're not going to start acting up like *that* little girl.'

My friend tells me that she felt as though she'd been slapped round the face. She's fifty now, but she's never forgotten the moment. She says that her father is a really good and kind man, but that he's just unable to show the love he undoubtedly has for her.

This is typical ESP behaviour. The ESP will rarely tell you that he or she loves you. In a moment of extravagant fondness an ESP might say: 'All the best' at the end of your phone call to him. But 'love' – never.

ESPs never tell you that you look nice or that they're proud of you. If someone else says: 'You must be so proud of your talented daughter', the ESP will shuffle from one foot to the other before muttering something like: 'Don't know where she gets it from.'

If you try to arrange some really nice treat for an ESP, and you phone to tell him about it, he'll never respond by saying: 'That would be really great, I'd love that.' Instead you'll get an answer like: 'Yes, I'm here that day. That will be all right – I should think.'

And don't waste your money taking ESPs to a posh restaurant for that special treat as they'll probably feel embarrassed at its theatricality and become even more introverted than usual. Worse than that, they won't even try to enter into the spirit of the place, and they'll hate the food and make it obvious they're having a miserable time. You will then feel that old familiar sense of crushing disappointment, so you're guaranteed to have a lousy time too.

So, for your own peace of mind, you should avoid these emotionally draining occasions. You're not going to alter your parents, so just accept that they are unadventurous folk who like to be socially invisible. Remember that happiness comes from putting right what you can and accepting what you can't. You can't change the character of ESPs. *They* could change if they wanted to – but they don't.

The ESP may be quietly extremely fond of you, or feel great pride in your achievements – it's just that he or she can't say so. One ESP I know collects all his journalist daughter's cuttings. But he's never said to her, 'Jolly good. I'm proud of you.'

This is the major problem with being the offspring of ESPs – you cannot help but wish that you had started life with more affirmation or more demonstrable love.

Sometimes it helps to look at the sort of upbringing your parents had. Sometimes you can see why they turned out so buttoned up – but not always.

The children of ESPs have to forge a way through life without any help from their parents. They have to do a lot of work on feeling good about themselves, and they have to learn to give themselves permission to feel more intensely about things than their parents appear to. They also need to feel OK about being demonstrative and throwing their arms around people and behaving extrovertly if they want to.

The alternative is to end up as an ESP – and who would want to do that?

ESPs are annoying, infuriating and lacking – and they fail their children. If the child of an ESP really wants to succeed in every way that his or her parents didn't – and many of them do want this – they have no option but to put their past behind them and bravely bound into life like an enthusiastic puppy. This is the only way they can counteract the inhibiting force of their family. And frequently, children of ESPs do become the life and soul of the party as they learn to compete with all those confident folk whose parents approved of, and affirmed them.

If you're the child of an ESP, your success in a career or in a relationship might well help you to forgive your hopeless parents and even to think quite kindly of them. Their failings – unlike those of some of the other types of parents in this section – are not malicious. And that's important to remember.

However, in order to catch up with your life and to live it fully, you may find that you cannot give much time to your parents. You may also feel that no matter how demonstrative you become with your partner, friends and children, you can never spontaneously throw your arms round your ESPs. That's the sad outcome of living with parents who, for whatever reason, were simply not good at filling up your emotional bank.

Most people who come to realise that they have ESPs do not exclude them from their lives – even if they limit the contact. They try to understand their mum and dad, who are generally very decent people in their own way. But there's no doubt at all that these offspring have been short-changed and that they feel it.

Surprisingly, children of ESPs often make fantastic parents because they consciously choose to make a much better job of the whole parenting process than their mother and father did.

The clinging parent

When you're an adult 'child' of a clinging parent you'll be familiar with a whole range of sayings that demonstrate how vital you are.

While most of us on phoning our mothers get this kind of greeting: 'Hi, Chris. How are you, love?', a CP will greet you with: 'Oh my God, it's you darling! Thank heavens . . . thank heavens you've called.'

This is normal language from a CP. It does not betoken a crisis or anything approaching it, but probably just means that you're ten minutes later than usual with your twice-daily phone call.

'So long as you're happy, I'm happy,' is another favourite expression which is usually uttered by your CP in a pained, strangulated voice.

A CP is often a mother – but not always. She frequently acts like a little girl herself and likes nothing better than for you to act all strong and treat her like a child. Furthermore, if she's married, she'll probably have trained her husband to treat her like a delicate infant. When he does that, they rub along well, but when he needs her to be a grown-up, she'll probably fall apart. The CP is actually pretty pathetic all round – especially in the home: some CPs do no cooking, others never take decisions.

The CP – whether male or female – will compete with his or her marital partner for your attention. And if you dare to spend time with your other parent your CP will sulk, or pick a fight with you.

The CP can often seem very generous. Brenda's mother, for example, wanted to loan her daughter £50,000. This was to help her buy a much better flat in London than she could afford on her own. Unfortunately, Mum expected to have a permanent room in that home so she could spend more time with her daughter.

Brenda was torn between having a nicer place, which she could never have called her own, and staying in a poky flat which at least was fully hers. In the end – and very bravely – she decided against the loan. Needless to say this choice caused a tidal wave of grief in her CP.

The CP always believes that he or she has your best interests at heart. This is rubbish of course. The CP will bribe, cajole or emotionally blackmail you to go to university near home, rather than allow you to go to the one at the other end of the country that you favour. She will also tearfully entreat you not to go travelling, and not to marry that particular partner, and not to take promotion if it means moving away. In other words she always puts her interests before your advancement.

As for Christmas, if the CP hasn't got a commitment from you by about February that you'll spend the whole of the next festive season with her, then she'll whinge and wail till you give in.

The CP will rarely like your boyfriends, girlfriends, or long-term partners. She'll constantly tell you that these people aren't good enough for you – but what she really means is that she resents your emotional involvements with other people and perceives everyone else as a threat to her closeness with you.

So, what can you do if you've got a CP? Well, you can train him or her to be different. I know this sounds a bit like teaching a puppy to be obedient, but it does work and I've helped several of my clients to do it quite successfully.

What you do is this. You reward your CP with contact when the CP behaves well, and you hold yourself back when he doesn't. So, when your CP behaves as a responsible and sensible parent should do, you give him or her lots of attention and praise. But when the CP is hysterical, and overwhelming and obsessive and neurotic, you keep your distance. Furthermore you work out how much contact you wish to have with your CP and you train him or her to accept that.

The absent parent

With two out of four current weddings in Britain destined to end in divorce, there are a hell of a lot of 'absent' parents these days.

I said earlier that there's not much point in apportioning blame for bad parenting, but there are a lot of divorced people of both genders who just walk away from their commitments as mothers or fathers – and it's not surprising that their kids feel hostile to them as a result.

I remember doing a television programme about a ten-year-old boy who was being offered for adoption. The reason he was 'available' was almost unbelievable: both his parents had remarried and neither wanted him now that they had new relationships. That little boy did find a new family, but I often wonder whether he ever really got over his natural parents' brutal rejection of him.

But APs hurt their children in less dramatic ways too. Only last week I heard about a divorced dad who'd promised to take his fourteen-year-old lad fishing for half-term week, but who cried off at the last minute and took his new, young wife shopping in New York instead.

These kinds of absent parents deserve to lose their kids' love – and frequently they do.

However, in many divorces, a person can find himself cast in the unsympathetic role of absent parent, simply because his spouse makes it almost impossible for him to see his children. This happens so frequently that a large majority of divorced parents who are not living with their kids, lose contact with them within a year of the family home splitting up. These parents are almost always men.

Through the years, countless guys have told me that they have arrived to collect their offspring – as sanctioned by the courts – only to have their ex-wife tell them that: 'Johnny doesn't want to come with you.' Or: 'Mary wants to play with her friends today.' Or: 'Susie's got a sore throat so I'm keeping her in bed.'

All too often a man might drive a hundred miles or more to see his child only to be turned away from his ex's front door. When this happens it's almost impossible for him to determine whether the excuses are genuine. But once he's been rejected in this way a few times, he often gives up. And he rarely finds out whether his children knew that he tried to see them, or whether they were told: 'Dad's abandoned you and is never coming back.'

I've even heard of a father's Christmas presents to his son being destroyed by the child's mother just so she could persuade her son that his dad had forgotten him.

But the final nail in the coffin of the father/child relationship often occurs when Mum gets a new boyfriend. Frequently, for convenience, the children are encouraged to use her new man's surname, and their real dad is forced further out of the picture.

It's possible that you have an AP as the result of your parents' divorce. This is very painful, and you probably feel aggrieved and miserable about it. But before you rule this parent out of your life and your emotions, do try to find out if he, or she, was an AP through intention or circumstance.

Many adults have met up with a parent they hardly know, and have gained a huge amount of love, affirmation and comfort as a result. So I do think that an AP should always be given the benefit of the doubt, because that act of kindness on your behalf might lead to a reconciliation that is very sweet and special.

So far I've been talking about parents that become APs as a result of divorce. But there's another type of AP – and that is one who has stayed married to your other parent.

These APs are people who are simply not good at family contact – especially when there are emotional difficulties in the house. Indeed, their customary method of dealing with awkward situations is not to deal with them!

These APs are almost always men. And they tend to take cover when things aren't going well.

If, for example, such an AP's marriage is going through a rough patch and his children are reacting badly to all the stress in the house, he'll most likely leave home at dawn every day and not return till bedtime. Then at weekends he'll have two rounds of golf to play, or a motorcycle rally to attend, or he might simply disappear to his workshop at the bottom of the garden and lock himself in.

I was talking to a highly stressed young man recently and I asked him whether he could discuss his feelings with his father. He replied: 'My dad's a good man – but he's just never there . . .'

I'm afraid that such fathers miss out on closeness with their children, and their kids find it hard to open up to them and indeed to forgive them for what feels like neglect.

If you had this kind of AP, it might help you to try to understand why he behaved as he did. Some offspring of such APs do renew contact with them in adulthood and find this rewarding. But this action requires a lot of forgiveness and maturity – and you may not feel able to make that effort.

On a positive note, as with the children of emotionally stunted parents, the children of APs often try extra hard to be better parents than their parents were – and many of them manage it. So lessons can be learned and some good can come out of all that pain.

The jealous parent

The jealous parent can be a nasty piece of work. Whereas most of the other pretty hopeless parents I've described – with the possible exception of the self-obsessed parent – are quite well-meaning, the jealous parent rarely has the best interests of his or her children at heart.

I'm afraid that the JP is often female – though some JPs are male. Male JPs tend to leave their daughters alone, but they're phenomenally jealous of one or more of their sons.

A male JP will pick on his son unmercifully. He will berate him if he's not good at sport. He'll bully him if he doesn't study enough. He may well vilify him if the lad is artistic, and will almost certainly mock him if the boy's a gentle, sensitive soul.

What all of this is about of course is the closeness between the mother and the son. If the father feels left out, or that he is not part of the bond that exists between his wife and offspring, then his jealousy will prompt all sorts of inappropriate and unkind behaviour. And if his hapless son turns out to be gay – as some lads who are close to their mothers are – then the JP will usually make the boy's life such a misery that the youngster will leave home at the earliest opportunity.

A male JP with a rampantly heterosexual son on the other hand frequently feels unreasonable jealousy at the boy's burgeoning sex life and opportunities. For this reason, he'll keep the boy short of money, and criticise his appearance and continually carp about how late the boy stays out. And should anyone try to make a joke about the old stag and the young stag, the JP will definitely not see the joke.

Sometimes this kind of relationship between father and son can improve in adult life, but only if the son can be bothered to try to understand his dad and to forgive his unreasonable behaviour. Some sons are prepared to jump through hoops to accomplish this, but not all.

The female JP is often pretty hopeless at relationships. It's not uncommon for her to have had several marriages/lovers. And if you're the child of a JP, you'll probably recall a succession of men passing through your house that you were encouraged to call 'daddy'. You may also recall that if 'daddy' got too fond of you, or took your side in arguments, then all hell would break loose.

You may have felt as a child – and indeed you may have all sorts of residual feelings of hostility about this – that your mother should have put you first, instead of her 'man of the moment'. And personally I think your feelings are justified. Crumbs of affection are of little consolation when some strange grown-up is getting the whole loaf.

Now that you're an adult it's almost certain that your female JP cannot abide your youth and attractiveness. Because of this she'll frequently spoil your joy in yourself at critical moments. A favourite ploy is to say: 'What's that on your chin? Oh – it's a tiny, tiny spot. Don't worry, I shouldn't think too many people will notice it . . .'

Anybody who can confidently sail out on a date after this kind of confrontation must have cast-iron emotions!

Indeed, a JP can be so resentful of her own child that she seeks out serious ways to inflict pain.

Bryony is a client of mine who came to me because she had had a termination two years previously. It had happened at a time when she hardly knew the lad who was to become her husband. But now that she had married him and they were settled and happy, the thought of this 'might-have-been' baby was haunting her. So she was mixed up and very emotional.

She was also hurt and confused because her mother was forever phoning her to talk about babies. This JP could not make a call without dredging up stories of Bryony's old school pals who were having their first or second children. It seemed she couldn't leave the subject alone.

'I'm sure my mother doesn't *mean* to hurt me,' Bryony said through her tears one day.

But as we talked, it became apparent that Bryony's mother had always deeply resented her child. And in typical JP fashion, Mum was jealous that Bryony's life was easier than hers had been. She also envied Bryony's intelligence and career and successful marriage – particularly the marriage, because her own relationships had never lasted for long.

In other words, this JP was a confused and bitter person who could never see past her own jealousy – which was eating her up – to rejoice in her own daughter's life and achievements.

The more Bryony talked about her mother's attitudes and criticisms, the more she came to realise that, on some level or another, her mother did actually want to wound her. This desire may well be unconscious but it still hurts like hell when you're on the receiving end of it.

As the weeks progressed, Bryony began to examine her mother more closely and to look at her motives. For the first time she talked about dark periods in her childhood when she'd been farmed out to aunts or put into boarding school.

And why had this happened? Because Mum had been in love with a new bloke. 'This is going to be *the* one', she would say and Bryony would be kept out of the way in case she queered Mum's pitch, or worse still, stole any of the attention that Mum so desperately wanted.

Uncovering these half-remembered memories was a painful process for Bryony: she cried a lot and kept saying that she wished she could have had a different mother – one whom she might have depended on.

But after a few sessions, the miserable hold of her past began to lessen its grip and Bryony emerged stronger and happier. She said she had at last uncovered her 'real' mother and that, somehow, now she'd faced up to the unpalatable truth, she could take control of her own life.

We discussed how she might do this really effectively. And Bryony came up with the idea of 'divorcing' her JP.

What this involved was purely mental – she didn't plan to rush round to her parent and tell her that she would never see her again. Instead, she made a decision that, in her mind, she would no longer consider her JP as her mother.

'I don't need all this pain and jealousy,' she told me, 'and I'm not going to let her inflict it on me any longer.'

Bryony then set about deciding how much contact she could cope with – now that she no longer had to think of her JP as a mother.

And she came to the conclusion that she would see her JP once a fortnight, but never spend another night under the same roof.

She then wrote down all her gripes about her mother on a very large piece of paper. We looked at them together and she told me that she was going to go straight home with this list and burn it in the garden.

Over the next few weeks I saw Bryony grow into a much happier and self-reliant person. Of course she still has regrets about her childhood, but she has made a conscious decision not to let them rule her life.

Going back over her past hurt her a lot. But that hurt was not as bad as the constant niggling ache she'd endured since childhood when she'd known that things weren't right with her mother, but had never had the strength to ask herself why.

Bryony is going forward. She understands her past. She's not letting it rule her life and she's taking responsibility for her own future.

Last time I asked her about her mother, Bryony told me that everything was 'cool'.

Though Mum obviously doesn't know that Bryony has 'divorced' her, it's clear that something significant has changed in their relationship. Mum seems much more 'together' and for some reason has started improving herself and reading self-help books. (I hope she doesn't read this one, or she may get a shock!) Mum also emails jokes to Bryony and seems much happier – perhaps it's because so much tension has gone out of the contact between them.

And Bryony said: 'I can see her for what she is and accept that. She's not going to change. So I don't get worked up any more.'

Bryony has learned a lesson that we all need to grasp. We can't change our parents, and we can't change the past; but we can change how we feel about it and we can certainly change ourselves, so that we don't allow our painful history to ruin our future.

Chapter Nine Key Points:

- Our parents have no right to expect more love and respect from us than they gave us.
- Examining what sort of parents we had helps us to understand our feelings for them.
- We can't change our parents.
- We can't change our past.
- We *can* change how we feel about our parents and our past.
- We *can* change ourselves so that the past stops damaging our future.

10

Happiness Comes from Balancing your Body, Mind and Spirit

Fifteen-year-old Ben sits in his room for hours on end. He's very moody and rarely goes out, except to school.

He spends most of his time playing computer games or surfing the Internet. He's a very fussy eater and will only eat burgers and beans.

He's got acne and is extremely spotty. He's clearly very miserable about this. His parents are worried about him, because he used to be quite a gregarious boy with plenty of mates.

Julia lives in a small town where she's the local librarian. Because of cuts in the library service, she's the only member of staff.

She lives alone: her parents are both dead and she doesn't get on with her only sister. She's lost contact with the friends she made at school and college, and has never replaced them. She spends her evenings alone – reading and listening to music. She's very unhappy.

* * *

Jason runs his own PR agency. He's twenty-seven and is determined to be a millionaire by the time he's thirty. He races around from morning till night – working very long hours and then drinking and clubbing.

He doesn't have a girlfriend, because he believes that a relationship would get in the way of his ambition, but he has loads of mates and surrounds himself with them at every opportunity. He hates being alone. He drinks 'far too much' but puts that down to the stress of his occupation.

He believes that only the tough survive, and has no time for anyone who can't keep up with him. He has several pet hates including the homeless. In fact if he's approached by someone begging in the street, he flies into a rage.

Jason feels sad much of the time, but can't understand why.

Emily is sixty-seven. She has an elderly mother of ninety who lives with her. Mother is remarkably hale and hearty – but something of a tyrant and Emily feels very 'put upon'. She has no job and rarely leaves her mother's side, except on Sundays, when she drives several other old people to church. Sometimes she feels that her life isn't worth living.

Doug is a publican, who works long hours in his pub. He takes no exercise outside of it and all he eats is convenience food washed down by around fifteen pints of beer a day. He also smokes heavily.

Doug has various sayings like: 'Salad is for rabbits', and 'Exercise is for wimps'. He never has more than five hours sleep a night because he 'relaxes' by sitting up drinking when all the customers have gone. He often gets very morose during these late-night sessions.

His wife is an alcoholic and no longer helps in the business. He says she drinks all the profits.

Sally is a fitness instructor at her local gym and leisure centre. She weighs herself several times a day and is constantly on a diet. She is wafer-thin, but seems convinced that she's several pounds overweight.

Sally's hobby is the same as her work – sport, sport and then more sport. She does several aerobic classes a day and plays squash and tennis. And if she doesn't also swim at least a mile a day, she claims to feel ill.

Exercise gives Sally a 'high' – but the good feeling never lasts long. She frequently feels that her life is empty and pointless.

Ben, Julia, Jason, Emily, Doug and Sally live very different lives but they have two things in common:

* they all feel unhappy;
* their lives are completely unbalanced.

Let's look at each one of them again.

Ben is a young man who needs help. Unfortunately, like many teenagers, Ben finds it difficult to talk to his parents right now. But they should let him know that they're concerned about him, and also suggest that he might chat to another close adult: a favourite aunt or uncle might be acceptable, or an older sibling or teacher.

This person needs to help Ben to find more balance in his life – and when he does, he'll feel happier.

So is Ben just going through a typical teenager's phase? Or is it more serious than that?

Well, I'm afraid it may be. A sudden lack of balance in an adolescent's life can sometimes indicate the onset of a psychiatric illness. This may be as commonplace as mild depression or anxiety – but it could be much more serious, like schizophrenia. So when a teenager starts acting like Ben, parents should always take advice from their GP.

Hopefully, the reason for Ben's moodiness and solitude may turn out to be much less dramatic. In fact, his skin may well be the culprit.

But though acne is not nearly as worrying a condition as schizophrenia, parents should still take it very seriously. Teenagers – and indeed much older people – can get so desperate about their spots that they become suicidal.

Nowadays, there are really good treatments for acne. There's also a brilliant support group – details in the directory – so there is absolutely no reason why a spotty youth should remain spotty. The first step, again, is to get Ben to his GP.

Another common reason for youngsters like Ben suddenly to turn in on themselves is bullying. If this is happening to Ben, it's small wonder that he seeks sanctuary in his room and is reluctant to face the world. Again someone needs to draw him out about this possibility, either to rule it out or to start dealing with it.

I doubt if many fifteen-year-olds will read this book, but plenty of parents of fifteen-year-olds will. So if you've got a Ben at home, please assure him that you're 'on his side' and then do all you can to help him get some balance back into his life.

Adults are different. They generally have to take responsibility for balancing their own lives. At the moment, Julia's lifestyle is completely unbalanced because her hobbies and her work are so closely entwined. She also spends far too much time completely alone and indoors.

My advice to Julia would be to retain her interests, but to make them more sociable. It will take some effort, but then change always involves effort and energy. It's also frightening, but if Julia is determined enough to balance her life and find more happiness, she'll take that risk.

A good way for Julia to mix with more people would be to apply for a job in a larger library – even though this would involve daily commuting to another town – where she'd meet other librarians with the same love of books as she has.

She spends too much time inside, so an outdoor hobby would balance things up a bit. Rambling would be a good option as lots of walkers are quiet, thinking people just like her.

She's interested in music, so I'd like to see her going to more concerts and, once there, to make it a habit to chat to at least five other concert-goers. And so long as she can sing in tune, she could get a lot of satisfaction and company by joining a choir.

She might also consider holidays or short breaks where she could meet folk with similar hobbies. There are music weekends in hotels up and down the country. Or if she's interested in thrillers and crime novels she'd probably enjoy one of those Murder Weekends which are great fun and really get the participants talking to each other.

Like Julia, Jason's life is totally unbalanced. But unlike her and Ben he doesn't spend nearly enough time alone. On top of that, he's totally self-centred.

He likes being in a crowd, but strenuously avoids relationships. Why is that? Maybe he has problems with one-to-one intimacy. Or maybe he's just too selfish to want to be involved with a real person.

But if Jason continues to avoid commitment and love, he'll wake up one day to find he's left romance too late and that lifelong love has eluded him. So my first suggestion to him would be to loosen up a bit socially and let himself be stirred by a pretty face, or a sultry voice, or a great brain, or, perhaps more importantly, by a kind spirit.

Second, I'd like him to re-think his 'me-first' attitude. Frankly, I find his views on the homeless distinctly unnerving, and I'm convinced that he'll never find genuine happiness while he remains unmoved by the plight of people in need.

He would do well to realise that truly successful people – those who are happy in their own skins as well as being high-achievers – generally balance their wealth and good fortune by investing in others.

I heard recently that the top tennis player Goran Ivanisevic donates $50 to his charity for Croatian children every time he serves an ace – which seems to be every other ball! He's clearly a man who seeks balance in his hectic life.

Jason should take a leaf out of Ivanisevic's book. If he doesn't actually want to go and meet disadvantaged kids at the local youth club, he could at least sponsor a child overseas. In return for a small monthly payment he would receive news of that youngster's progress and might derive some sense of pride from seeing his money make a tangible difference to someone who has nothing.

Jason also needs hobbies. Drinking or clubbing aside – and they're probably not doing him much good – he seems to have no leisure interests. In any event his drinking is undoubtedly contributing to his gloomy feelings, as alcohol is a depressant. And his consumption is likely to take a toll of his physical health in time, if he doesn't take steps to reduce it.

I'd like to see Jason do some solitary swimming, where he can just think and be – this would be a great change for him. I'd also like him to drive to the seaside and walk, alone, by the tumbling waves and just let his mind wander. But most of all I'd like to see some evidence that he has a heart tucked away in his manly chest, instead of a lump of stone.

Ambition is great, but if people fail to balance it with other characteristics and values, it can lead to a hollow and unhappy existence.

Emily is different again. She's a doormat – and doormats always get trodden on. Somehow, she's let herself get into a completely unbalanced situation over which she has no control. In fact she's living a non-life and exists only as the daughter of her dominant mother, or as 'that kind lady' who drives pensioners to church.

Deep inside herself, Emily doesn't feel much like 'that kind lady'. The truth is that she's seething with frustration and missed opportunities. But she dare not express such emotions, so she bottles them up and consequently feels even more hopeless and miserable.

She frequently wishes that her mother were dead, but then spends days agonising over her wickedness at thinking such a thing.

Emily needs to take control of her own life. It's no use waiting for her mother to die – she needs to do something *now*.

Emily has a brain and she has free will and it's time she used them.

She should begin by seeking advice from Social Services about respite care for her mother in the short term, and also about day-to-day care and domestic help on a permanent basis.

Then – and this would take a lot of courage – she should arrange to take a holiday, without Mum, somewhere lovely, warm and sociable. And on her return, she should get out more and build a life of her own.

This won't be easy at first: living under her mother's thumb has sapped her confidence – but little by little Emily should be able to construct a proper balanced life for herself and start to feel much happier.

Obviously Mum won't be pleased if Emily makes these changes, but after moaning a lot, she'll probably get used to it. In fact, she may even develop some respect for her daughter for standing up to her, and also for seeking a balanced life at last.

Doug, the publican, is a mess. He does have one thing going for him in that he has a bit of balance between being with others and being alone. But other than that, his lifestyle is chaotic.

Doug is a drunk – a victim, you might say, of the business that he's in. But there are plenty of publicans who drink sparingly or not at all. There are plenty of publicans who run marathons, or get to a gym three times a week, or take their dogs out for long, brisk walks. There are also plenty of publicans who eat salad. And there are plenty of publicans who get a good night's sleep. So if he really wanted to, Doug could change his life and find some balance.

Granted, Doug also has to contend with his alcoholic wife, but he can't blame all his troubles on her, because most of them are self-inflicted. Doug is a perfect example of an unhappy person whose sadness is caused – to a large extent – by the fact that he doesn't take care of his body. It's very, very difficult to feel good and happy when your physical self is wrecked through booze, smoking, lack of exercise and a surfeit of junk food.

My best advice to Doug would be to start by getting serious help with his drinking. Alcoholics Anonymous would be a good choice.

Once his mind is less befuddled by drink, he'll be in a better position to make changes elsewhere in his very unbalanced existence – and these should include more exercise, a better diet and a real go at kicking the nicotine habit.

He might also decide whether or not it's worth trying to persuade his wife to get help, or whether to call time on that relationship.

Doug can make all these changes and clean up his act – if he wants to.

* * *

And finally, we come to Sally. Her lack of balance shows that you can definitely have too much of a good thing! We all need to take exercise, but her quest for fitness has ceased to be healthy and has become obsessional.

As for her diet, she's no longer just keenly watching her weight – she's got an eating disorder. I'm afraid that Sally is on the verge of becoming quite ill and she needs to help herself by getting help urgently. Her best bet is to see her GP and to tell him or her exactly what's going on. I would also advise her to contact a support group for people who have problems with their eating habits (details in the directory).

Naturally I would suggest to Sally meantime that she takes on more nourishment and that she cuts down on her exercising; but I fear she may be so gripped by her compulsions that she's unable to make these changes on her own.

However, with good professional support, Sally can turn from the unhappy woman that she is currently, to someone who eats normally, exercises normally, enjoys a wide range of hobbies and has a social life.

Getting to that point will not be easy for her. But so long as she admits that she's in trouble and seeks out the help I've suggested, there's no reason why she shouldn't triumph over her problems, and learn to balance her life effectively.

Over the past few pages, I've outlined six very different stories of unbalanced living. And I don't suppose that you had any problem spotting where each of these people was going wrong! But now you need to turn the spotlight on yourself and ask if there are any similarities between you and the above individuals – and if so, what you're prepared to do to improve the situation.

You can certainly follow any of the relevant advice outlined above. But I'm going to give you further help in identifying your imbalances and sorting them, by taking you on a journey through those areas in life where we tend to get things out of proportion.

Drinking
Non-alcoholic drinks

If you want to feel good physically and mentally, you must take in sufficient fluid. And the best fluid is water.

Water is a great beautifier. Look at the skin of anyone you know who drinks lots of the stuff and you'll see that it's clear and fit looking.

In fact, to stay healthy we should drink about eight glasses of water a day. This takes some doing at first, but with time and persistence it becomes a happy habit as opposed to a chore.

You'll know that you're drinking enough water when your urine is almost colourless. This is good news for your body. But did you know that pale pee is also a sign of happiness?

Frequently, when we feel irritable and grotty, we're actually dehydrated. And quite often when we reach for food – in the belief that we're hungry – we're really thirsty instead. This means that a glass of water will make us feel much better than the bar of chocolate, or the biscuit, we thought we wanted.

So, if you want to feel happier, remember to drink your eight glasses of water every single day.

Of course most of us seek comfort from all sorts of other hot and cold drinks – and that's fine. But they shouldn't replace the water ration.

As for the other fluids, well, you do need to strike a balance between still, sugarless drinks and those cans loaded with fizz and sugar.

It's also important not to overdose on caffeine. We all know that magical moment when only a cup of strong coffee will do. It gives us instant 'get up and go' and clears our minds. But too much caffeine – more than about five cups of coffee daily – can make us jumpy by day and wakeful by night. So balance your intake with more water, or with decaffeinated beverages.

Alcohol

Vast numbers of unhappy people drink too much booze. They frequently know that they drink too much, but they feel that their current difficulties justify their indulgence.

I certainly don't want to be a killjoy. After all there's a wealth of enjoyment to be had in a crisp gin and tonic at the end of a working day, or in a glass of full-bodied red wine sipped and savoured in the company of your friends or partner. But it's a different story when drinking controls you, rather than you controlling it.

Often the problem is a temporary one, while the person struggles with sadness or excessive tension or strain. But we all need to keep an eye on alcohol intake, because it can get out of hand.

When I have clients with anxieties about alcohol, I also give them a little test to do. Much to their surprise, I never ask them to *stop* drinking! You see, problem drinkers can almost always give up booze completely – for a while. What they can't do is drink in moderation. So I ask them to try rationing themselves.

If you're worried about your drinking you might like to try the test too.

All you do is this: you go out for a jolly evening with friends and you have two drinks. Then, you allow someone to buy you, or pour you, a third one – but *you don't drink it!* Instead, you must push it to one side and go on to mineral water or anything else non-alcoholic.

For someone with a drink problem, this is almost impossible. And plenty of my own clients have come back to me to report that they were quite unable to manage it.

If you can't, then you should accept that your drinking is beginning to control you – and you need to do something about it.

Of course when people are unhappy, the last pleasure they want to give up is drinking. I understand that. But often, as in the case of Doug, the drinking is actually exacerbating their unhappiness. This is partly because of alcohol's inherent depressive effect, but it's also because most people secretly dislike drinking too much and feeling that they're not in charge of this aspect of their lives.

One last thought on booze: when people stop drinking, or learn to control their alcohol intake, they generally find that the benefits of being sober are much more widespread than they'd ever imagined. Their minds feel clearer. Their memories improve. They frequently find that eating healthily becomes easier, and that they stop getting themselves into unwise sexual situations, or spending too much money.

In other words, too much alcohol leads to a very unbalanced lifestyle. Sort the drinking – and much of the rest of life will balance up too.

Eating

Unhappy people often find it very difficult to eat well. Some folk find that their misery leads them into eating empty calories for comfort. Others find that feeding themselves becomes a chore and they gradually lose their appetite.

Our moods, our energy and our systems are directly linked to what we consume, so it makes good sense to fuel our bodies properly.

Often unhappy individuals say that they opt for junk food because preparing and eating healthy foods takes too much effort. I always ask such people to do just one thing, which is to add five pieces of fruit to their daily diet – even if the rest of it is fry-ups or takeaways! This gives them some vitamins and roughage – and as they begin to feel the subsequent good effects they frequently feel encouraged to make other improvements.

There's no doubt that many unhealthy foods clog up your system, and I defy anyone to be cheerful if they're constipated. In any event, constipated people usually have constipated attitudes like meanness, bitterness and self-righteousness. The unsavoury reason for this is that people who hang onto their own waste products tend to hang onto their unhealthy mental baggage too. So a sluggish system means a sluggish, troubled mind.

People with efficient systems on the other hand are generally much more carefree, expansive and cheerful! They also feel lighter and more energetic – and they have far fewer colds and other illnesses.

So you can do yourself many favours by eating well. And one way to encourage yourself to do this, is to work at developing a habit of 'wanting' good nutritious food.

You see, it's very difficult to pick the good option when you're mentally labelling it as boring. So when you're choosing food in a supermarket or restaurant, try never to say: 'I suppose I *ought* to have the salad.'

'Ought' is one of the most dreadful and despairing words in our language – and it's calculated to make us want to do exactly the opposite. If you think that you 'ought' to order the grilled fish, you'll either pick it, and feel cheated, or – more likely – you'll ignore your inner voice and select deep fried cod and extra chips!

When you say instead, 'I'd love the grilled fish', or, 'That fruit salad looks delicious', the chances are that you'll order and eat them with relish!

There's never been such a variety of healthy food so readily and so cheaply available. And if you shop late in the day, you can guarantee to get good reductions in fruit, vegetables and other perishable foods every single evening in superstores, and in local fruit and vegetable outdoor markets too.

Getting the happiness habit is all about being responsible for yourself and caring for your mind, body and spirit. Eating well is a special part of this process, so it makes sense to treat yourself to healthy and enjoyable foods.

You are what you eat, goes the old saying, which is absolutely true. And a more balanced diet will lead to a more balanced you.

Exercise

Just as with food, try to eliminate the words 'should' or 'ought' from your vocabulary when you're talking about exercise. You will never keep up an exercise regime if you feel you 'ought' to do it. So, whatever you try to accomplish in the form of exercise, for goodness' sake pick an activity that you like, and which you've therefore got a chance of continuing.

A lapsed exercise programme is much like a lapsed diet. It makes you feel more depressed than you were before you even tried it. So, don't set yourself up to fail: instead choose realistic and enjoyable goals.

Your aim should be to do something energetic enough to get your heart racing three times a week for twenty minutes at a time. You may be thinking that a certain amount of sex should do it.

But I want you to regard that as an extra!

Obviously jogging, swimming, tennis, squash or circuit training will fit the bill. But if you know that you frequently give up on such things because you never seem to have the time, money or inclination for them, then you might do better to build more exercise into your everyday routine.

You can soon get the habit of always walking up escalators in stores or at stations. You can easily leave the car at home and walk to pick the kids up from school. Or you can make it a rule to walk up the stairs in an office block rather than queue for the lift. Getting off a bus or train a stop before you reach home is also a good way of building physical effort into your day.

Exercising is very important. It encourages good bone density. It also strengthens your heart and lungs and, most importantly for people seeking the happiness habit, it releases endorphins. These are chemicals in the brain that help you feel good.

People who are physically active invariably feel much perkier than couch potatoes. They also feel proud that they are caring for themselves, which also helps to feed the happiness habit.

Sleep

In recent years it's become fashionable to believe that you can get by on only five or six hours a night. But a recent report showed that this belief is rubbish. Apparently most of us don't function at all well unless we have eight hours.

Certainly, more and more people nowadays think that they're unhappy, when actually they're exhausted. Lack of sleep is the enemy of health, energy, libido and feeling good. So if you know that you regularly short-change your slumber, then find some way of remedying the problem. Within days you'll feel more alive and content and you'll realise that the bard was absolutely spot on when he wrote about 'Sleep that knits up the ravelled sleeve of care'.

But suppose you have good intentions about having plenty of sleep and you get off to sleep OK, only to wake up feeling that you've got the world on your shoulders at around 3.00 a.m? If this is happening to you, I urge you to see your doctor. This pattern of sleep disturbance is indicative of depression and you may need some medical help to overcome it.

Another sleep problem is doing it to excess. Now, most busy people can't imagine what that feels like, but take it from me that too much shuteye is as detrimental to your happiness habit as not getting enough.

When people are unemployed, or depressed, or suffering from poor self-esteem, or working in boring jobs, they quite commonly take to their beds complaining that they're always tired.

The truth is that they're tired with themselves and with their boring lives, but they're not genuinely fatigued at all. Over-sleeping is unhealthy and can only make you feel sluggish, headachy and fed up.

So if you know that your life is lacking in action and stimulus, and that you do seek refuge in sleep, please get your act together and do more.

For example, if you're unemployed, it's a good idea to try to structure your day so that you get up at the same time as you would if you were working. This helps you feel much more productive. It also gets you to the Job Centre early, or to the library – where you can read all the situations vacant columns in the newspapers before your competitors happen by.

Similarly, if you're a freelance with insufficient work, try to get up at a respectable time. Then, after just a quick cup of coffee, do a few letters pitching for jobs before you have your bath and breakfast. Feeling that you've made a start at an hour when you're normally just dragging yourself from the comfort of bed helps you to feel more businesslike and considerably happier.

Getting a structure into your days takes guts and energy, but it does help your sleep patterns. And getting the appropriate balance between sleeping and waking feeds your happiness habit.

Company – adults/children/friends/partner/alone
You're unlikely to feel happy if you fail to balance the company you keep.

If you only ever see colleagues and no friends – then a vital part of your social network is missing.

Similarly if you've dumped your pals, because you're so in love with your partner, your social life will have a great gap in it.

And if you have plenty of adult company, but don't see enough of your children because of your working hours, you'll feel that you're missing out – and you'll probably feel consumed with guilt too.

As for time to yourself – that's important too. In fact, we all need some time to call our own, or we tend to feel constantly rushed, and at everyone else's beck and call.

It's especially important to find time for yourself when you're a mum – something that many mums fail to do.

Take Serena. She used to have a demanding job in banking until she stopped work to look after her twin babies.

When the children were about six months old, Serena's husband realised that his wife no longer had any time for herself, so he took a day's leave and encouraged her to go off on her own for a few hours.

She was quite excited as she took a train into London, but she was undecided about how she should spend these precious few solo hours. She wanted to enjoy herself, but she felt strange away from home and the twins, and she couldn't think how to occupy herself.

Eventually she went into a department store and bought two little dresses for her babes and a sweater for their dad. Then she caught the next train home – much to the amazement of her husband, who couldn't understand why she wasn't making the most of every free moment.

It took this weird experience for Serena to realise that she had forgotten how to be a person in her own right. In the space of a few months she'd changed from being an independent woman with friends and hobbies, to a stay-at-home mum who existed only for her family. Having seen how unbalanced her life had become, Serena started booking baby-sitters more regularly so that she could get out alone – and also so that she and her husband could have time together without babies.

So, do you spend enough time with your friends, your partner and your children? Do you also have enough time on your own? Have a close look at your life. What you find may surprise you.

To help you to see the picture even more clearly, I'd like you to draw up a list of all the people who are important to you and then to give them a rating according to how often you see them.

- Give them 5 if you see them too often;
- Give them 4 if you see them more than other people;
- Give them 3 if the balance is about right;
- Give them 2 if you don't see them as much as you'd like;
- And give them 1 if you see them so rarely that you really miss them.

Once you've marked up your list and have seen where the surpluses and the deficits are, then you can begin to get some healthy balance into your social life.

Working/leisure

Few of us nowadays can expect to have as much leisure as we'd like. But it's vital to have some.

There is no doubt at all that people are working longer and longer hours. Roffey Park, the management institute, surveyed a thousand adults drawn from all sections of the UK economy, and they discovered that 96 per cent of these individuals believed that working extra hours is expected nowadays.

This long-hours culture is seen by many people as the key to success. In fact it has become so much a part of our lives that in some firms employees are accused of skiving, or of taking a half-day, if they dare to leave before six.

Now, it is possible that at the start of a career you can get by with little sleep and leisure in a bid to ensure promotion. But you can't keep up with this kind of crazy schedule. If you do, you'll be all washed up and wrung out before your time.

So, if you work very long hours, you must learn to maximise your leisure time. You need to preserve your weekends – and definitely not take work home to catch up. You must also take your full holiday entitlement: there are no medals to be had for working through your vacations. Remember too that no one will congratulate you on all the long hours you've worked if you have a nervous breakdown. The powers that be are much more likely to see you as an embarrassment and inconvenience.

So look carefully at your lifestyle and try to balance it better.

This also applies if you're a freelance worker. It's common for people working for themselves to find it almost impossible to switch off at weekends or to take holiday periods. But some leisure at these times is essential if you want to find the happiness that a balanced life can bring.

It's also important to balance the *type* of working life you have with a different kind of leisure.

For example, it's not going to do you any good at all if you're an accountant by profession, and then you spend your weekends helping your kids with their maths homework and doing the paperwork for your wife's business.

You should be out hang-gliding, or running, or surfing instead. Even if you're not a very sporty person, you should still balance an indoor job by getting out in the evenings and at weekends.

And if your job is sedentary, it's wise to balance it with physical activity in your leisure times. Let's face it, if you sit at a computer all day, the last thing you should be doing at the weekends is playing computer games or wandering the web.

By balancing your type of work with a suitably different sort of leisure, you'll establish a healthy equilibrium, which will feed your happiness habit.

Frankly, making appropriate changes to improve the balance between work and leisure is often just a matter of common sense – and yet people the world over fail to make the effort to effect the changes that would propel them into a more pleasurable existence.

Spiritual/practical

At the beginning of this chapter I wrote about Jason and how his 'me-first' attitude to life was one of the barriers to fulfilment and happiness for him.

He had two similar problems: he had no consideration for others, and he never made time in his life for the quiet feeding of his soul.

In other words his life was entirely practical with no provision at all for the spiritual.

Many individuals nowadays claim to have no faith in any structured religious system. But whether or not organised religion is for us, we do all have a spiritual dimension – and this needs to be nurtured.

It's possible to find it in a church, even if you have no Christian beliefs. A shadowy corner in an ancient cathedral evokes strange stirrings in even the most prosaic of souls.

Secular buildings with historic connotations can also provide a sense of wonder or mystery that opens up our inner beings.

I remember visiting a house in Vienna where Mozart had once lived. It was a magical feeling to look at the walls and then out of the window and to know that I was sharing views that the composer had seen as his mind filled with the sounds that he would write during his short lifetime.

I felt breathless with excitement and deeply touched to be able to experience – even in a very different century – the same space as this incredible, creative genius. Even as I write these words – some fifteen years afterwards – my heart beats faster and I know that my soul was touched forever by that visit.

Other experiences that reach and feed our souls include walking by the sea; listening to great music; lighting candles and repeating a mantra; sitting in a peaceful garden.

In a sense, I don't think it matters what you do, so long as it gives you space to clear your mind, and food to fuel that deep, most inaccessible place which is the essence of your being.

When you spend this kind of spiritual time alone, for a start, you motivate yourself, and you can see more clearly which direction you should follow.

Second, you put yourself in touch with the people and things that matter to you. For example, you can feel close to someone important to you who has died. Or you can feel touched by a loved family member who lives too far away for you to see them often.

Third, you develop a sense of being 'at one' with the rest of the world and its people – and through this feeling of collective fellowship you may well come to assume more responsibility for others.

It's so easy in our modern world to feel that we have no money or time for people in trouble. Instead we're usually moaning on that we don't have a second bathroom at home, and we can't afford a conservatory. Indeed, we may be so bound up in our futile materialistic race that we never pause to consider how well off we are. The truth is that no matter how poor we feel, we're all in the top pointy bit of the world's pyramid of wealth. And the majority of our planet's people would certainly perceive that we live in untold luxury compared with them.

Being aware of our good fortune changes our attitude from being entirely self-serving into a feeling that is more real and more responsible.

And with these new emotions we discover a different kind of satisfaction, fulfilment and happiness.

So whether or not you think you're a religious person, take care of your soul. This is the real you, and unless you serve it, happiness will elude you.

Chapter Ten Key Points:

- Balancing your life is essential if you want to be happy.
- Happiness comes from eating a healthy, balanced diet.
- Happiness comes from finding a balance between:
  1. being indoors/outdoors;
  2. privacy and company;
  3. quietness and noise;
  4. being with family/friends/adults/children/partner/ colleagues – and being alone;
  5. what you do for a living/what you do for leisure;
  6. being active/being inactive.

11

Happiness Comes from Bidding Farewell to the Unhappiness Habit

Getting the happiness habit is difficult enough, but breaking the unhappiness habit can be even harder. So over the next few pages, I'm going to give you some final tips about dumping the sort of unhelpful thoughts and phrases that we all use, but that stop us moving wholeheartedly towards a new and happier life.

Among the most stupid and counter-productive sayings that we – especially women – repeat with monotonous regularity are 'I shouldn't be having this', or 'I shouldn't be doing this.' Mostly we use these phrases in relation to food – especially at pudding time.

I admit I've been known to utter these words myself, and I've lost count of how many times I've heard friends and colleagues use them. But this kind of self-indulgent guilt is crazy. Worse than that, it spoils our own pleasure and infuriates others. So next time you're wondering whether or not to treat yourself to a 'sinful' dessert, for goodness' sake either have the blessed thing – and resolve to enjoy it wholeheartedly – or give it a miss. Remember: a happy person doesn't need to play these barmy games.

'I don't deserve such happiness!' is an equally damaging phrase, even when we don't say it aloud. It's certainly common for insecure or unhappy people to *think* it when they're in the throes of a new relationship. And these thoughts can become so overwhelming that they jeopardise the fledgling romance.

So if you know that you go around feeling undeserving, please remind yourself that if *you* don't think you deserve happiness, no one else will think it either.

Unfortunately, our worries that we're undeserving don't stop at love and relationships; they also extend to our careers.

Again it's the fair sex who have the major problem here. We frequently feel like impostors if we're promoted. Sometimes we even feel guilty that we've triumphed. And we tend to fuel these feelings with thoughts like: Oh God, they'll find me out in a minute', or, 'They must have been bonkers to have given the job to me.'

This skewed thinking can get out of hand and ruin what should be wonderfully joyous feelings of achievement.

Of course, you wouldn't be human if you didn't have some reservations about a new job. You might even decide that, having got it, it's not what you want after all. That's your prerogative, and it's OK. But it's very definitely not OK to go into the 'I don't deserve it' routine. You do deserve it – just as you also deserve happiness.

You deserve compliments too, and an individual who's got the happiness habit is able to accept them graciously. Furthermore, a happy person feels affirmed when someone says her hair is great, or that her dress is stunning; and she's able to repay her complimenter by smiling graciously and agreeing with that person's judgment.

So from this moment on, how about eradicating phrases like 'Oh, that old thing' when someone likes your outfit. Or 'It needs cutting actually' when they praise your hair. Or 'I'm really fat and gross today', when a friend admires your slim figure.

Remember that when someone bestows a compliment, he or she

can feel quite hurt to have it challenged or disregarded. In fact you'll find that if you keep repelling favourable comments, people will stop making them.

So do yourself – and everyone else – a favour by consciously accepting compliments with smiling grace. Someone who has the happiness habit appreciates him- or herself – and can also enjoy appreciation from others.

Another thought that will stop you finding your true happiness habit is when you decide that someone, or something, is *making* you unhappy.

You hear people complaining like this all the time. 'He makes me so unhappy,' they say. Or ' My job makes me miserable.'

But the fact is that *you* are responsible for your happiness – no one else. It's certainly possible that your relationship may be going badly and that you feel depressed as a result. And it's equally likely that you're in the wrong job and, consequently, feel diabolical. But these things are not *making* you unhappy. You are *choosing* to be unhappy because of them. You, and you alone, hold the key to your own happiness and unhappiness.

So if you're ever in a situation where you're tempted to believe that something or someone is making you miserable, take matters into your own hands and make the necessary changes that will help you feel happier.

I began this book by asking how you'd feel if you suddenly discovered that you were going to die today.

You'll know you're truly content when you can answer: 'I'd be very sorry, because I love life. But I've given it my best shot, and I've made it my business to enjoy it as much as possible.'

It seems to me that the happiness habit is like one of those perpetually moving chair-lifts at a ski resort. You can feel quite anxious at the thought of committing to it. But then you summon up the necessary effort and courage, and jump on. Sometimes, just for a second, progress is slow and a bit juddery, but suddenly the whole thing gains momentum and you find yourself laughing with sheer exhilaration as you're swept up and away.

Of course, you could just watch other people get on the ski-lift while you debate whether or not you've got the guts to join them. You could let the first chair go, and another, and another . . .

But that's not the way to have fun. Is it?

UK Directory

I've divided this directory into two parts:
- an A to Z of where to get help;
- recommended books.

An A to Z of Where to Get Help

Abortion (Termination)
British Pregnancy Advisory Service (BPAS)
Tel: 08457 304030
www.bpas.org

Post-Abortion Counselling Service
Tel: 020 7221 9631 (24-hour answering service)
www.pacs.org.uk

Also see *Coping with a Termination* in 'Recommended Reading', below.

Acne
Acne Support Group
Tel: 0870 870 2263
www.m2w3.com

Activities and education

If you're interested in participating in a new activity or learning something new, try the following:

Ceroc – tel: 020 8846 8563; www.ceroc.com

Department for Education and Skills – tel: 0870 000 2288; www.dfes.gov.uk

Learn Direct – www.learndirect.co.uk

National Federation of 18 Plus Groups – tel: 01531 821210; www.18plus.org.uk

Open University – tel: 0870 900 0305; www.open.ac.uk/firststep

Ramblers' Association – tel: 020 7339 8500; www.ramblers.org.uk

Alcohol problems

Al-Anon Family Groups – support for family members, colleagues and friends of problem drinkers
Tel: 020 7403 0888
www.anonuk.org.uk

Alateen (part of Al-Anon) – support for young people affected by a problem drinker.
Tel and website: as above

Alcoholics Anonymous – groups throughout the UK. See your local phone book for the one nearest to you.

Aromatherapy

Contact the Aromatherapy Organisations Council for details of an aromatherapist in your area:
Tel: 0870 774 3477
www.aocuk.net

Assertiveness training

Capita Learning and Development – runs excellent courses in assertiveness.
Tel: 0870 400 1000
www.capita-ld.co.uk

Also check with your local council's education department or with your public library for evening/day classes in assertiveness in your area.

Anxiety and phobias
There are a number of excellent support groups for sufferers including:

No Panic – tel: 0808 808 0545; www.nopanic.org.uk
National Phobics Society – tel: 0870 7700 456;
   www.phobics-society.org.uk

Bereavement
Cruse Bereavement Care – runs a national helpline and local groups, and has lots of excellent publications.
Tel: 0870 167 1677
www.crusebereavementcare.org.uk

Conciliation services
These provide help for separating and divorcing couples so that they can sort out arrangements for their children and property:

Family Mediation Scotland – tel: 0131 558 9898;
   www.familymediationscotland.org.uk
National Family Mediation – tel: 0117 904 2825;
   www.nfm.u-net.com
Solicitors' Family Law Association (SFLA) – tel: 01689 850227;
   www.sfla.org.uk
UK College of Family Mediators – tel: 0117 904 7223;
   www.ukcfm.co.uk

Counselling/psychotherapy
This is a general list and does not include specific counselling for alcohol problems, eating disorders, post-termination depression, relationship or sexual difficulties: these categories are all listed separately.
   There isn't much counselling/psychotherapy available on the NHS apart from some counselling in GP practices, and some provision for 'talking therapies' within psychiatric units.

However, there is significant help available in the voluntary section, and the best organisation to contact about it is:

MIND (The National Association for Mental Health)
Tel: 0845 766 0163
www.mind.org.uk

The majority of counselling and psychotherapy in this country takes place in the private sector. Here is a list of organisations who will provide you with the names of qualified practitioners in your area. Their websites enable you to search for a local therapist by using their online database.

British Association for Counselling and Psychotherapy
Tel: 0870 443 5252
ww.bacp.co.uk

British Association of Behavioural and Cognitive Psychotherapists
Tel: 01254 875277
www.babcp.com

British Psychological Society
Tel: 0116 254 9568
www.bps.org.uk

National Council of Psychotherapists (which represents many psychotherapeutic approaches)
Tel: 0115 913 1382
www.nationalcouncilofpsychotherapists.org.uk

United Kingdom Council for Psychotherapy
Tel: 020 7436 3002
www.psychotherapy.org.uk

Depression
Depression Alliance – publishes useful leaflets and acts as an umbrella organisation for many different support groups and mental health associations.
Tel: 020 7633 0557
www.depressionalliance.org

Meet-A-Mum Association – for women suffering post-natal depression.
Tel: 020 8768 0123
www.mama.org.uk

Divorce and separation
National Association for the Divorced and Separated
Tel: 01692 583358
www.divorceandseparation.org.uk

On Divorce – an important source of friendly support and a means of easily accessing information and experts.
www.ondivorce.co.uk

Domestic violence
Women's Aid National Helpline – for women in jeopardy from physical, verbal and mental violence.
Tel: 08457 023 468
www.womensaid.org.uk

Eating disorders
The Eating Disorders Association
Tel: 0845 634 1414 (adult helpline) or 0845 634 7650 (youthline)
www.edauk.com

Hypnosis
National Council for Hypnotherapy
Tel: 0800 952 0545
www.hypnotherapists.org.uk (includes an online directory)

Massage

British Federation of Massage Practitioners – can give details of a qualified masseuse or masseur in your area.
Tel: 01772 881063 (24 hours)

Massage Therapy Institute of Great Britain – will supply names of practitioners who trained with the Institute.
Tel: 020 8208 1607

Meditation

Friends of the Western Buddhist Order (London Buddhist Centre)
Tel: 020 8981 1225
www.fwb.org

Transcendental Meditation
Tel: 08705 143 733

Rape

Rape Crisis Federation
Tel: 0115 900 3560
www.rapecrisis.co.uk

Rape and Sexual Abuse Counselling
Tel: 01962 848024
www.rasac.org.uk

Relationship problems

Relate – there are branches of Relate throughout the UK. Counsellors will see couples – straight or gay – or people on their own who want to discuss their relationships.
Tel: 0845 130 4010
www.relate.org.uk

Alternatively, see your local phone book for a branch of Relate near you.

Couple Counselling Scotland
Tel: 0131 558 9669
www.couplecounselling.org

Relaxation tapes
Most health shops or chemists sell excellent relaxation tapes.

Sex aids
Passion8 – a mail-order company run by the effervescent and well-informed Stephanie Taylor.
Tel: 01482 873377
www.passion8.com

SH! Women's Erotic Emporium
www.sh-womenstore.com

Sex problems
(a) NHS
There are NHS psychosexual clinics in many big hospitals up and down the country. To get a referral to such a clinic, see your GP.

There is also free treatment available in some Family Planning Clinics throughout the UK. These are staffed by specially trained doctors who not only know all about contraception, but are also experts in all manner of sexual problems like premature ejaculation and vaginismus.

Find details of your nearest clinic in your local phone book. You don't have to go through your own GP; you can simply contact the clinic direct.

(b) Private sector
British Association for Sexual and Relationship Therapy
Tel: 020 8543 2707
www.basrt.org.uk

Some of these therapists are also medical doctors, but the majority of them are lay counsellors with special training.

Institute of Psychosexual Medicine
12 Chandos Street
Cavendish Square
London W1G 9DR
Tel: 020 7580 0631

The members of this Institute are all medical doctors who specialise in treating sexual problems. Ask your GP to refer you. Or you can contact the Institute direct.

Sexual abuse
NHS: there is NHS help for adult survivors of childhood sexual abuse, so please do see your GP about this.

Rape Crisis Centres: your local rape crisis centre will also be a source of help. They will know about counselling, support groups and group therapy in your area. See details on p. 202.

Survivors for Men – this is a support group for men who have been sexually abused as children.
Tel: 0845 1221 201
www.survivorsuk.co.uk

Also see the book *Breaking Free* in 'Recommended Reading', below.

Singleness – returning to being single
Single Living (formerly Single Again) – offers advice, support and friendship opportunities for people who find themselves returning to single status.
Tel: 020 8762 9933
www.single-living.com

So You've Been Dumped
Tel: 08707 425 315
www.soyouvebeendumped.com

Single parents

Families Need Fathers – a support and action group for dads whose relationship problems have resulted in difficulties with seeing their children.
Tel: 020 7613 5060
www.fnf.org.uk

Gingerbread – provides day-to-day support and practical help for lone parents.
Tel: 0800 018 4318
www.gingerbread.org.uk

National Council for One Parent Families
Tel: 0800 018 5026
www.oneparentfamilies.org.uk

Suicidal

The Samaritans – are there at the end of a phone, 24 hours a day, 365 days a year.
Tel: 08457 909090
www.samaritans.org.uk

Yoga

British Wheel of Yoga
Tel: 01529 306851
www.bwy.org.uk

Yoga for Health Foundation
Tel: 01767 627271
www.yogaforhealthfoundation.co.uk

Either of these organisations will tell you about yoga teachers in your area. Your local library may also have these details.

Recommended Reading

Anorexia Nervosa: A Survival Guide for Families, Friends and Sufferers by Janet Treasure. Psychology Press, price £9.99.

A Woman in Your Own Right: Assertiveness and You by Anne Dickson. Quartet, price £6.00.

The Big 'O': Understanding and Improving your Orgasm and Your Partner's by David Delvin and Christine Webber. NEL, price £6.99.

Breaking Free: Help for Survivors of Child Sexual Abuse by Carolyn Ainscough and Kay Toon. Sheldon Press, price £12.99.

Bulimia Nervosa and Binge-Eating: A Self-Help Guide by Peter Cooper. Robinson, price £6.99.

Coping with a Termination: Advice on the Emotional and Practical Difficulties of an Unwanted Pregnancy by David Haslam. Vermilion, price £6.99.

Overcoming Anxiety: A Self-Help Guide by Helen Kennerley. Robinson, price £6.99.

Overcoming Depression: A Self-Help Guide by Paul Gilbert. Robinson, price £7.99.

Overcoming Panic: A Self-Help Guide by Derrick Silove and Vijaya Manicavasagar. Robinson, price £6.99.

Overcoming Social Anxiety and Shyness: A Self-Help Guide by Gillian Butler. Robinson, price £7.99.

Women's Pleasure: or How to Have an Orgasm . . . as Often as You Want by Rachel Swift. Pan Books, price £9.99.

Index